REDISCOVER YOUR MIDLIFE MOJO

REDISCOVER YOUR MIDLIFE MOJO

NANDITA KAUSHIK

NU VOICE PRESS

First published by NU VOICE PRESS 2024
An imprint of Hubhawks Pvt. Ltd
www.nuvoicepress.com

This is a work of fiction. Space and time have been rearranged to suit the convenience of the book. Except for public figures, hotels, and institution names, any resemblance to persons living or dead or the real events are purely coincidental. The opinions expressed in the book are those of the characters, and should not be confused with that of the Author.

ISBN: 978-81-966888-5-1

Typeset by Saanvi Graphics, Noida
Printed at Thomson Press
Published by Nu Voice Press

Appreciate and laud your successes, big or small

Contents

PART TWO
UNRAVELLING THE RAMBLINGS

PART THREE
ACTIONS

PART FOUR
THE GRAND FINALE
NUGGETS OF WISDOM

Introduction

THIS book started out as a reactionary tale to the myriad of middle-aged ramblings in my head—you know, those vague mutterings and irrational thoughts that somehow make sense. So, instead of verbalising them and giving earfuls to hapless listeners, I decided to vent by writing them down.

Conversations with my mates (others of this decade) yielded a resonance with the ramblings, so based on that small yet validating sample, I started to pen down our middle-aged, long-winded, and slightly verbose journey.

Just to clarify, I am dedicating most part of this book to those aged 40–58 years. Any older decades could be kept aside for my next book when I hit that road.

Coming back, this entire demography is more or less ignored. These "sandwich" ages of 40–58 years are squeezed between making both ends meet—expenses of growing children, their education, marriage, etc., and the needs of parents, often financial too. This weary group can tend to be non-glamorous, not really able to put on too many fake smiles or claim that life is zestful and inspiring, till, of course, you find that perfect trade-off between time and work. Oh, and to add to the list of tasks demanding life force energy is, exercise! Now how does one fit that in?

By now I am sure you have either nodded in agreement or dismissed it all, saying, "It is not so bad, you know. We do party, have fun, socialise, drink, dope, whatever." Well, either reaction is fine, but either way there are times when you want to reach out to a kindred soul in the form of a book that does not relentlessly demand more success, more dream fulfilment, and more life-draining tasks out of you.

Of course, this book is ageist, but since a middle-aged person wrote it, I am forgiven, I think.

Shared with you are glimpses of middle-aged life, partly based on my own experiences, partly on observations of the lives of others and what they asked me to write. Empathy with some action is what this age seeks, and hopefully at least some of the pieces in this book will make you feel more at ease with yourself and your age band. All I hope is for a few nods in agreement, a few smiles, but many relating to the pieces.

Just one word of advice—please read the book slowly, a piece at a time. Take your time, mull over each article, chew over what you agree and disagree with. That is all I ask.

Hopefully, I can see you nodding at how the midlife world suddenly looms in front of you changing every paradigm as described in part one of the book. How sandwiched you feel, how your body and money start relating a little differently, not to mention how the midlife crisis hits you from nowhere, how new and old friendships provide some relief, and how all is not lost when empty nests get regurgitated with new relationships.

That takes me to part two of the book, all is not lost, in fact, if anything, it is the start of a new innings, transformed with positive action and intents. Usher in the new you and enjoy the liberating relief of midlife. When philosophy kicks in, wisdom wins the day, actions are revitalised and the middle-aged sits down invigorated to enjoy all the revelations, cross-examinations, and new learnings that flood him/her. Making sense of all the revelations and enjoying the new sides that emerge as a result, the middle-aged will get ready to live life more meaningfully and more deliberately.

Once the philosophies have been philosophised, the wisdom been shared, and laurels of revelations enjoyed, it's time to set things in motion. How will this happen, what will be the new ways of living and the small, everyday moments that will be created? After all, this intense introspection must result in some useful actions, right? The third part of this book presents some actions for you to undertake. Feel free to discard, adopt, adapt, or modify as deemed fit!

The last part contains "Nuggets of Wisdom". Each letter addressed to the youth discusses a small but important shift from the popular or accepted norm. These new norms form the nuggets or tiny pieces of wisdom that the middle-aged can share with those a generation behind.

This book has short, disparate chunks empathising sometimes humorously and other times seriously, covering the everyday and the macro, the surreal and the mundane—but with no epitaphs or formula for success. Interspersed with personal experiences and values, the book just aims to be a gentle, meandering, empathic companion as you walk through the various stages of life seeking validation that maybe, just maybe, you are on the right track.

Before the end of the yester-years, is the newness of resurrection

HERE I sat, looking out of the window of my balcony, absent-mindedly observing the usual humdrum of life. There were damp clothes hanging—drying and "purifying" (as per grannies' tales)—on wire under the relentless rays of the Delhi sun. Women stood chatting across balconies, no doubt sharing cooking or maid-handling tips, even indulging in a bit of husband-bashing. I felt the frustration and fatigue of the gardeners, the labourers working hard to make the world a little better for people like me. The everyday life of making money and breaking one's back while making it.

Inevitably, when life pauses for a while in the mad middle-aged rush, I indulge a little in daydreaming and drift off to the private garden within. The scenes I see of the outside world dissolve into a disembodied slow motion. As one ruminates—milestones, dreams, the years gone past—an important facet of this journey has also been relationships—the central pain and pleasure of mankind.

As you look back, you notice that some journeys come with a destination and an end point. In some cases, the people stay but the relationships go, and in others, the people go, yet the relationships linger on. Which one is better? Debatable. But everything does change and lucky are the relationships that change as people do and manage to stay in perfect tune.

This, my friends, is the core of the middle-age—a stage where introspection is thrust on you, where you try to make sense of the past moments eventually steering to a new future.

It is that extremely uncomfortable time of facing things best left alone, saying things best left unsaid. Yet we know that discarding old imprints is the first step towards creating new footprints. It is that time when you question almost everything, including the face you were born with. But here is the bright spot—you pretty much know or can anticipate most things. You arrive tumbling and rumbling, and end up emerging, if not victorious, at least wiser.

Enough said; let's begin this journey…

PART ONE

A SANDWICHED AGE: THE JOURNEY

… Arriving jostled, bewildered, and tumbling to the middle-ages

1

Discovering The Middle-Ages

HOW do the middle-ages greet you? Once you have arrived, what are the immediate indicators? Is it when the laborious days take over or when the world forgets you exist? Better yet, maybe it's when the mind operates with a will of its own and you realise you are an authentic fake person.

My midlife discovery? When procrastination felt like an entitlement and not an ailment! I chose to step off the fast track and was happy to procrastinate possibly everything except putting out my mental fires. Discover your midlife discovery in my ramblings...

The demands

You peek out of the door, ready to hide at a second's notice. What exactly are you hiding from? Demands! Caught as you are and sandwiched between the young (your almost grown-up children) and the old (your rapidly aging parents), not to mention your own existential crisis—midlife, career stagnation, wrinkles, and minor aches here and there—I reiterate, this is not an easy decade.

The days are packed between proving relevance at work, pretending to be completely in command of your senses all while last night's binge-watching catches up with you (that was the only me-time available). You force close attention to work decisions, data, issues, since you are in the commanding seat, trying to keep abreast with all the automation and processes launched in the office at earth-shattering speed. Not to mention the team expectedly looking up to you to somehow handle the latest irate client, the market that just will not respond, and the colleague who won't deliver.

The good news is that by now you know all the short-cuts, the actions, the decisions, and the words that would handle all these issues in milliseconds. The bad news is that it's one more thing you are expected to do, and let's not even mention all the things waiting for you at home.

The almost grown-up kids await your purse/wallet once you reach home, the elderly parents are waiting with their list of tasks for the evening, and your spouse, if you have one, is caught in her/his own set of tasks. Driver duties could also be added to the list. Then the bills, the college dues looming large, and while peering at your online bank account, of course with your reading glasses on, you gloomily prepare the budget for the month or the quarter, depending on your resources. The silver lining? You know how to postpone some possible issues, and how to block a few others, and "hmmmm" your way through most conversations, thereby reacting only to the urgent and important ones.

Exercise, the gym, or power yoga almost seems like a cakewalk and a definite escape till you start gasping for breath, trying to win the ever-losing battle against weight gain. Again, a consolation—now you know better and have lowered your expectations multi-fold. You are also very strategic—exercise hard the day before any medical tests so the doctor thinks you are in the pink of health.

In short, life has taught you the tricks, smart work, and smart thinking needed to deal with it. An important trick? Timing. By now you have learnt when some things are better left unsaid, waiting for an opportune moment to plunge the dagger of relocation or quitting your job to enter entrepreneurship. Monumental decisions that need a resting pause.

Well-hidden for later are your fantasies. When you visualise the retirement age, when you travel the world, lie on beaches and deal with the occasional hiccups, such as keeping track of interest rates on your investments, the real estate rates, premiums of the medical insurance for your family...all in a day's work. After all, life has been a great teacher.

Yes, you have reached middle-age...the early indicators?

You know you are middle-aged when your child's career excites you more than yours. Yes, this is a true indicator that you, my friend, have turned a corner. I caught myself at a recent get-together waxing eloquent about my son's promotion, and it went slightly beyond a mother's pride. Bored faces, polite smiles, and the restless drumming of fingers drove me to the fact that the Everest-like climbs of my son had my listeners wearing thin.

And I realised that I was getting a voyeuristic pleasure from peeking into my son's future more than my own!

Of course, we are relieved when our children climb the pinnacles of success, but there is a thin line between applauding their limelight and climbing onto their lit bandwagon.

Something akin to those Bollywood moms trailing their naive daughters through the movie sets and taking control of their career, money, roles—you get the gist.

While we do encourage and support their endeavours, we also owe it to our grown children to be their beacons of inspiration. As we are, they become. So, if we want them to be consistently successful, hardworking, or happy at their work, that is exactly where we need to be as well. Carrying our miserable laments to an uninspiring, dullard environment is not how they want to see us, right?

Just an ending note—you did good, kiddo!

More signs....

There are some signs that we need to recognise and accept for better peace of mind or sanity. These are given below in no particular order of importance. Some may call them psychological ageing signs or social ageing ones, to me, they are all biological ageing signs. That is the starting point after all.

- You are a little short on patience so grit your teeth as you drive your 90-year-old father who insists that slow driving is the only way to drive and regals you with often-repeated tales of driving prowess. His, of course.
- Fashion tips from the youth seem impossible to meet so you find it easier to just embarrass them.
- You understand and finally stopped expecting ego gratification from the immediate family, but the larger community steps in, thankfully. For the family, you are first and foremost a mother, father, sister, brother, etc.

and then anything more. All daddy and mommy issues of the youth become a thing of the past, thank God.

- You realise you are becoming a "mother" or nurse to your ageing husband/partner, and the same applies to men too—they become "father figures" or worse, "grandfather figures".
- After numerous cost-cutting economy flights, you have reached that income, designation, or stage when you stop flying economy or discount airlines. You have experienced the repercussions and think you deserve better now.
- Another compromise of the younger years that you halt? You stop taking the middle seat in the flight thinking it's a just a short trip—every minute is excruciating and if you are a woman between two over-fed men, it is catastrophic. So, you pay extra for that aisle seat and pretend like the other two do not exist.
- If for most of your life you have been a simple and straight person, you set the record straight now—do not assume there is no hidden diva in you or a "divus" (the male equivalent as per Wikipedia, drawing on the Latin term from the Roman empire using it in reference to emperors). When that diva or divus will emerge from the shadows is not in your hands, so might as well accept and give it the limelight it wants.
- Last but not the least, the traffic, weather, infrastructure, well, pretty much everything in life can be a source of potential stress, as you have learnt the hard way, so now you know which battles to pick.

Hey, we still exist!

While I am very clear that we, the middle-aged, have miles to go and many more lands to explore, both figuratively and literally, I am not sure whether the rest of the population agrees. Subtle ageism starts seeping in. To be honest, this entire book is ageist, as I am typecasting an age, right? But listen, only I can give myself the permission to do this, not the others! Here is what I am noticing on this journey.

What happens when you hit fifty years and start moving towards the wrong side of the fifties? Quite simply, you vanish, cease to exist, vamoose, disappear… get the picture? How can I say that? Well, the evidence is overwhelming…

- You disappear from market research surveys. Most age cut-offs are at forty-five years. After that, you are not expected to have a single lucid opinion, nor are you expected to make any significant contribution to ideas or purchases. May I remind you that according to the *AARP Longevity Economy Outlook* report, consumers aged 50 and above contribute $8.3tn each year to the US economy. Closer home I do see retail therapy, expenses on food and drinks, travel, and various looking good factors on the upswing—as a friend commented, "I can spend like a 52 to look like a 42."
- Most advertisements do not talk about you or include you in their audience unless they are a medical, insurance, or a housing brand! Really? Do you know who can afford the latest Iphone? Certainly not my 25-year-old kid and neither am I buying one for him. Well, to

be honest, the latest, most expensive phone in the house is with the one who knows the least how to use it—my 88-year-old brand-savvy father.

- The sales staff in retail outlets start talking to your adolescent son/daughter instead of you. Hey, who is paying the bill here? And guess who is starting Salsa classes soon? Cater to ME with all the latest leotards, dance pumps, and makeup to hide my perspirations as I gyrate to new steps.
- Makeup brands start wooing you with their anti-aging and anti-wrinkle creams/serums, swiping all other products of the table. Not to mention the hair-colouring aids and creams. I agree, we do need to hide more than we reveal now, but do you really need to be so cruel about it?!
- The worst are mobile brands. You cannot have friends, cannot be tech-savvy, cannot be fashion conscious—these territories only belong to the twenties and below. And no, contrary to popular belief, we are not imitating the younger ones, we are now zeroing in on value.
- Certain stereotypes start building in people's heads. If you are mid-fifties, you must be facing memory loss, figure loss, reduced efficiency, become more judgmental, stingy, and irritable—in short, you are stressful and unhappy. Hence the complete surprise if you happen to like trendy music, can still dance in the latest styles, still look physically fit, and have a youthful disposition. "Hey, you can't be all that—where do we go?" ask the youngsters.

- Then there is the uncomfortable time when you want to change career mid-stream or give interviews for senior positions. "Hmmm, you don't seem overjoyed when I asked about your availability for weekends and late nights" and "You seem a little too serious and set" or "I think you are a little more experienced than what we had in mind." So, courageously, you don't act your age, show your enthusiasm for late nights, woo your boss, and don't give your opinions unless asked—again, stay the way you were in your twenties and thirties.
- After forty-five years, you are either expected to be the CEO of a company or a consultant or a mentor—if none of these, you have not been successful in your career trajectory.
- Please don't expect to be easily employed if the age difference between you and your boss is a little too close for comfort.
- The work you get is inversely proportionate to your experience, and the zeal and energy of the youngsters is constantly compared to your silver hair—never mind the thinking. At least it was passable and on time.

So, folks, when you hit the fifties or the wrong side of fifty, you have two choices. Either you adjust and gracefully leave the younger ones to slug it out, or fight tooth and nail and hang in there by your fingertips. Of course, if you are the lucky, visible, and an in-demand fifty-year-old, then please do the others a favour—bring the mid-forties and fifties back into the limelight.

Did this piece hurt? Hey, I am just being a little crabby. After all, I am expected to be at this age. Wait, wait there is more—did I tell you about the time when I enrolled in a digital course…no? Here it goes…

One digital course for me please!

Determined to make myself savvier and more relevant to this digital world, I studiously researched for many courses and finally settled on one from a highly reputed institution, albeit a trifle expensive. Registering enthusiastically, attending all the welcome sessions, and finally unravelling the online portal that carried my name, I sat down to start work….

The first and a very embarrassing roadblock to even starting the sessions on my portal—I had to register my date of birth. I was stuck for two days as the infernal drop-down list ended at 1972! There was no option for anyone born prior to 1972. Half fuming and half laughing at my conundrum, it was fun watching the institution squirm with embarrassment as they corrected their mistake.

So, yes, we do exist.

Thoughts and I

Related to the need to show the world that we exist, is the bigger need to keep putting your best foot forward. After declaring we exist as productive brave members of society, I have a confession to make. In the privacy of my home study or the mirror in my bedroom, I can safely confess that there is one thing my growing years are frightened of—*the sheer volume of uncontrollable thoughts!*

Now, I have, since forever, a deep dislike for lists of any kind. In my not-so-humble opinion, I felt it was a waste of creative energy and was the modern way of boxing me and my life into neat little "To Dos". Also, it meant being organised and that just didn't suit my freedom-loving brain and heart.

So, imagine my shock when I realised that my brain secretly was making lists on an auto-pilot mode!

Terribly stressed by the overload of thoughts and ideas that kept whirling in my brain, disturbing the poor guy's sleep and down time, he decided unilaterally (the "he" is only for convenience) to receive the thought, analyse it for a few milliseconds (or whatever is the appropriate unit of time) and compartmentalise them into slots.

These are as given below, and for your ease, I am also giving a few appropriate examples:

- *Can be solved but not today*—food habits/concerns/ worries.
- *Cannot be solved today*—when will I need to stop waxing, dieting, dyeing my hair, etc.
- *Cannot be solved at all... leave it to divine intervention/ God/Universe, etc*—behaviour of current or ex-spouses/ partners, bosses, and related carriers of ill tidings!
- *Can be solved but not my problem till asked*—friends' romantic and marital problems
- *Need not be solved, this is a random thought which deserves to be ejected out*—did the maid clean properly? (this is a potential ulcer-creating thought and hence needs to be immediately evicted from the brain)
- *Need not be solved as it is none of my business and my opinion has not been solicited*—office gossip; office

politics and thoughts related to someone's weight, performance, looks, etc.

- *This is a good thought/idea*—to be preserved and repeated as many times as needed—kind peaceful thoughts, loving and positive thoughts celebrating self, current life, and relationships.
- *Urgent thought needs to be actioned immediately*—deadlines, house on fire, etc.

To my surprise, I realised that this is actually making my life easier…I now have brain-time for leisurely reading, sleeping, and even meditating without worrying about the impending deadlines! My only worry is what if each of the body organs decided their own lists. Can you imagine the chaos if the liver decided to act independently of the stomach for which foods it would process and which ones it would not, etc.

Oh well, this thought too goes down the list of *need not be solved, random thought…*!

What cannot be conquered must be faked

Despite the brain re-structuring your thoughts and you becoming steadier with your lists, there is one constant companion who never leaves your side as you grow. You would think you have outgrown it and no longer bear its companionship now that you are older and wiser, but alas, it decides to cling to you even more. What am I rambling about….?

Fears! Somehow this is the one thing that just cannot be conquered. But if it's any consolation, they keep evolving and a new list gets created every few years.

You just don't stop being afraid. The list can range from the inanest to the real deals.

So, what do you do? Rather than fight headlong, after all hitting your head against a wall only gives you a bumpy forehead, you fake the bravado. You look, sound, act brave—keep at it till you start believing it is the only way. And the best part is, not only are you able to fool yourself, but many others too. So, who says bravado is not a good strategy, for isn't it said that bravery is not the end of fears but moving past the fears? Bravado is that set of actions, that role-playing that you do to convince others till it becomes your second nature.

The dice is also cast around this age-decade. At the slightest provocation, you lose your digestion and temper. Would it not be better to not lose either of these very important functions to fears and insecurities but rather observe them from a microscope to recognise, not reform them.

It is also at this time that you empower yourself with acceptance. It teaches you what cannot be cured must be endured, and what cannot be endured must then be accepted. Bravado is accepting the cards that are dealt to you, accepting that you are an imperfect creation plagued by fears, and finally accepting that strength and vulnerability are not opposites, but uneasy companions that will co-exist almost all your life.

Procrastinating at its peak

So, what happens when you can't accept or fake or plan your thoughts and actions—you procrastinate!

I was late again. Despite all efforts, warnings, and alarms, I was going to miss that train by five minutes, a mere blasted five minutes as I rushed to travel to Connecticut for a job interview, no less. No number of self-recriminations, amount of self-disgust, or inner shouting was going to help me catch that train. And then, hallelujah! Arrived the Uber driver. He was not just any other cab driver, not because he knew the local trains like the back of his hand, I rejoiced something else about him. The words he said when he learnt the time of my train and how difficult catching it would be…

"We procrastinators must stick together and help each other," he said in complete understanding and empathy, smiling amusedly. Needless to say, he was middle-aged too.

Without blinking an eye, he set off in a new direction, determined to help me catch my train from a new station. His words stuck with me long after he had gone. For the first time, I felt understood. I felt someone intuitively knew and shared the pain of being a chronic procrastinator. Oh, by the way, I did catch the train.

So, what makes me and many others like me procrastinate? Is it a late rebellion of living on the edge—the challenge of not knowing if we will make it on time? Is it a continuing block against being disciplined and organised, or is it just a tendency to not take things seriously enough, including yourself? Maybe, it's all of these or just lack of exercise and sleep leading to a lethargic body. All valid but rather harsh judgments meted out by the more organised species.

Generously speaking, some of us procrastinate because we are in another world many times. Don't get us wrong, we are not lazy. Just caught up in our thinking, imagination, and creative world. We simply lose track of time as many ideas are blooming in the fertile mind simultaneously. Where is the time to get ready and go? Or have we learnt, by having been on time for most of our lives, delays can be precious too?

So, when this Uber driver accurately pinpointed the problem—procrastination—a part of me protested. What if I had a genuine reason? Maybe there was a fire, a mishap, a fight—why did he not consider any of these reasons or even grumble about passengers stressing him out? He just plain understood and calmly laid out the diagnosis, in sync with a phenomenon that no doubt plagued him as much as me. His reactions were quick; no point in pondering over the "ailment" or even bemoaning its causes—he just moved swiftly into Plan B. Now, if only the world behaved a little more like him towards us chronic delayers.

Late rebellion strikes

Here is a warning—those who have not had their quota of misadventures, indiscretions, sowed their wild oats, or just behaved like youth is expected to behave, they may do so in their middle-ages

Wait, hear me out—I am not saying the rebellion has to be of volcanic proportions or shaking the foundations, it could be a quiet seething, a tirade of complaints or just a sudden, unwarranted action. You know, akin to the last straw kind of rebellion.

The pent up has to be evacuated and hence the rebellion. Many who are controlled in their youth and are forced by families to live responsibly might want to shake loose. This is different from the midlife crisis—this is more in acknowledgement of wanting to experiment and live a little dangerously.

Those who have had their reckless fun may visit memories to make stories and yet others may realise that they do not have those stories to tell. So hey, let's live a little. Bolstered with a little alcohol, tacit agreement of fellow mates, this subset is on a roll for a little late rebellion.

I include within this set of arrivals, the late bloomers. I am not talking of celebrities alone, even the more commonplace amongst us who decided to write their first book at 50, or a corporate honcho who just quit one fine day declaring with a yawn, "I am bored," and here is what she did next—opened a dance school. Or the fine international journalist who shot to fame with a fan following from his YouTube travel videos. Or the crazy-nut who post-travelling 40 cities worldwide, rebelled against this nomadic lifestyle and opened an online platform from his elderly parents' home.

For those younger, who are snickering behind their hands, this is rebellion enough for us, just getting off the stable-salary bandwagon fills us with fear. Yet, there is a high-pitched "hyper-anti-authoritarian" instinct growing to pathological levels. Possibly embarrassing the now sedate youngsters or adult children around us. I remember the dismay on my kid's face when I bowed out of the corporate race. Hey! in my defence, I did not smoke (still don't), didn't drink (still don't), so a little unusual is fair game now.

Mostly, I think the underlying need is to become a more interesting person in our own eyes, resuscitate the stultified state that we have narrowed ourselves into. Be nice folks, we are just rebelling to finally fulfil our youthful yearnings.

And that takes us to the new conundrum—in the midst of our little rebellion, we try to rediscover the man/woman we left behind….

2

Deciphering the Middle-Aged "You"

BETWEEN the tumbling and the mind still coming to terms with the new phase, the question of your identity suddenly looms large. Almost as a precursor to the midlife crisis, the hapless middle-aged decides to start from the core, indeed a very good place to start. Maybe that's where it will all become clear. And maybe now we would at least start to grow. It is a little introspective, with some pontifications but bear with me, you will emerge lighter.

The journey to being stoic nomads…

As we experiment and uncover our real selves, the first realisation that hits us is the looming fact—life is changing all the time.

Stability is an illusion which only one species of nature—the human beings—clings to in a desperate bid to control existence. We make structures, processes, offices, homes, a career, bank balances—all with the confidence that these tangible evidences of our eminence will stand the test of time. Unfortunately, when we lose jobs, sell homes to fulfil goals, we lose that dream of stability too. What helps at this point is stoicism and the non-reactive flexibility of the middle-aged. We learn to simply pick up the pieces, find new jigsaw pieces to puzzle over, and move on to solutions.

Like the time I lost a dream-like job in a dream-like international destination due to internal politics. After ranting blue murder and raining abuses, I gathered my scattered dignity, faked on my stoic face, and moved on.

Borrowed from the animal kingdom is the survival instinct to keep moving to greener pastures.

Living in the moment, easy acceptance of a new reality, zero resistance to the instinct that says move, and hope that movement will lead to a new "forest" replete with resources—these are the mantras of nomadic middle-aged humans. Not that it is necessary that we are forced to become nomads. Some of us choose to relocate, start new roles, marry again or for the first time, adopt a child, and sundry other unprecedented yet happier choices. After all, the insulating comfort of stability can also be quite suffocating.

In this newly acquired nomadic mindset, do remember a little self-adulation. A pat on the back periodically reminds us that despite being nomads, we have also successfully juggled being middle-aged nurturers and providers.

Along the way, in true gypsy style, when we board our moving homes, we empty our backpacks, live light, and know that if change is the only constant, then at least we can control what we carry.

Who are you?

As an outcome of the growing introspective deciphering, you want to know—sans your personal and professional identity, who you are inside-out. Turning to psychological and other tests, you have a tough time answering close-ended questions or responding to single choice options because all situations or options at some time or another made sense and may have been faithful modus operandi.

As you gain more experiences in life professionally and personally, making or remaking a LinkedIn profile or even a simple visiting card becomes an excruciating task. While all these professional modes of identity help at the beginning of working life or for slightly more focused and singular-path human beings, they definitely do not work for a multi-tasking and multi-income sources person.

Fewer creative souls, artistic individuals, medical professionals, or alternate healing practitioners have a LinkedIn profile. How do you assimilate all the various ways in which these professions work into a single phrase that can aptly describe the skills and abilities of these professions? I mean, it is a little difficult for a creative person who is a painter, sculptor, writer, poet, potter, etc., to simply sum up their abilities. A lawyer may find it far easier to call himself or herself a lawyer, with maybe a specialising genre added on.

In a nutshell, after a certain age, it is more accurate to not try to answer the question "who are you" in close ended options. You are reassessing and probably realising that life needs a re-start. That the body you have been pushing with the same bursts of fuel, the goals that you have been chasing, and the pot of gold you have been seeing like a mirage at the end of the rainbow probably needs a re-visualisation.

As we re-assimilate and look at things that worked in the past—the patterns that need to be shed and the laurels we earned, it is important to weigh them metaphorically and see whether they still give you that surge of kick, or if there is room for new laurels. Maybe, the LinkedIn profile now needs an entire sentence to describe you and your career and cannot be summed up in two or three words. Maybe, you now have more skills to offer professionally and want to see multiple streams of work and income.

Why am I harping on about LinkedIn? Well, it is the professional face we show to the world. It boasts our achievements to a world that does not know how we reached our career pinnacles, so to some extent it is a bit of an understatement of who we really are. Equally it is true that people just want to know who we are today and what we have to offer, not really how we reached there.

Coming back to the question then—who are you today? Answer the probes below, and maybe you will know more.

- Are you the same person who embarked on this journey a decade back, and are still content with your status quo—workwise or in any other way? A deep introspection every nine years and a review/relook every five years would be enough to keep a check.
- The answer to the previous question leads to these consequential questions:
  - ↪ What new skills have you picked up along the way?

- What is the way you would describe yourself now?
- What new ways can you look at yourself, professionally and personally?
- At least workwise, is there something you have honed that others have not?

Many questions, I know, but anyone who has the courage to sit down and start scripting the answers is already halfway home.

Who are you? – part II

Have you been a "rolling stone", a "seeker", a "fossil", or somewhere in between all of these titles? This is the favourite way of the world to judge the middle-aged and gauge a person's potential and journey, professional or personal, by these terms. The youth, of course, are spared this fiery scrutiny.

Between the terms rolling stone and seeker, I personally prefer the latter. While a rolling stone has some negative connotations (you know, a rolling stone gathers no moss, et al), a seeker connotes a more positive, spiritual meaning. What each boils down to is a restlessness to not stay in situations or circumstances that are inert and non-stimulating.

Allow me to wax eloquent with some analogies. Neither water nor air is ever still. Both seek newer levels and force. So, a tiny stream flows into a river, which further flows into the mighty ocean—constantly seeking more powerful levels and a higher force. Air is never still; it can be in a state of a light breeze or have the ferocity of a storm.

Where I am leading to with all this rhetoric is that some people keep moving across different professional and personal decisions with the ease of an acrobat, while others prefer to stay long term quite easily in the same space/situation. You could be a "seeker" over a "settler". Since a settler is easier to recognise, let me talk of a seeker.

A seeker is a state of mind which makes life easier for one if he/she just accepts that as a part of their personality. For organisations, while a seeker is a bit of a problem, once recognised, they can be an asset. This is the individual who will carry out the more difficult tasks, crisis situations, complex topics, demanding clients, etc., as long as you ensure the person is evolving constantly and getting due autonomy and recognition.

Boredom is a complete no–no for the seeker, and you need to put up with some eccentricities, such as: "I need a break for unwinding, a sabbatical to just travel and explore." This affliction can happen at any age or time for them, but generally comes in full force as a part of the midlife analysis, or dare I say, crisis. Yet there is a difference between a rolling stone and a seeker. While the rolling stone gathers no moss and hence no learning, the seeker evolves and grows alongside.

The seeker's primary motivation is growth, while the rolling stone seeks just variety.

For the seeker, peace will come with the acceptance that they will experiment and may have short tenures in most positions unless a workplace/life partner/place is found that allows them to experiment within some broad boundaries. Only very secure individuals can stay with seekers, as they know these actions are not personal.

So, what does the seeker do?—keep seeking, knowing that change is the only constant. Learning from the past, but not staying there too long. No experiences or incidents were accidental; they both happened and ended for the same reason.

So, when discovering who you are, see which of the below-mentioned thoughts resonate with you…

- We are all individuals and will only work well in a team when we can relate to a common cause and our individual needs are met.
- No labelling is needed for anyone. None of us are born as team players or non-team players. These are nomenclatures given to place people in neat little boxes and make one sound better than the other.
- As children, we are taught to share and care for others and to work as classmates in a social setting. However, the unfortunate side effect is that we are also taught to conform and neglect our individual personalities.
- Consensus leads to order but it also represses innovations.
- As workplaces and as families, most optimum condition is to have "safe and comforting" environments but allow members to make unsafe and uncomfortable choices that lead to an innovative-thinking team.
- In the end, we are all responsible for being individuals working freely within a team, so don't wait for permission. Go ahead and create that environment.

We are being forced to "grow"

Assuming that a forty-five or even a fifty-year-old has grown to that age and what it entails is an erroneous idea. Many of us have just been putting one foot forward at a time and groping our way through. We imitate, observe, read, converse, and somehow learn how to take the next step, yet have we grasped, understood, and consciously created that step?—debatable.

As we read more and gain more knowledge, we realise how childish (and not childlike) we still are, how we still hanker after parents' approval and society's validation, despite being parents to adults or close-to-adult children. In the privacy of our bathroom, we desperately pray that we are making the right decisions.

We resist, we rationalise, and have fantasies. We project, we identify, and we dream. In short, we continue our journey of growth, yet we do not all fully realise how much we still need to emerge from our adult fears, childhood tendencies, and reactive inclinations. The good news is, again like introspection, growth also seems to be forced on us in our middle-ages.

Deliberately, we seek to differ from the generation above us, and yet grow to understand that the generation below us will do the same.

In time, we grow to understand which beliefs and attitudes no longer serve us, and in fact, are outright ridiculous for a middle-aged person to have.

We grow to become more selective with our social company, to be more politically correct, at least in speech, and behave in a manner appropriate for the grey, well, whiter, hair.

And those of us who are not on this journey, all I can say is heaven help the rest of us.

3

Midlife Crisis

AFTER that intense round of self-reflection, is it surprising that a crisis would be brewing inside? Many outside the middle-ages seem to associate midlife only with midlife crisis. While I do admit this is a fairly large episode among "midlifers", it is still just one of the many episodes that hit us. So, what exactly is the midlife crisis and what happens therein? A few hypotheses and descriptions might help decipher this black hole.

Hurtling to the proverbial crisis

No book on middle-ages would be complete without addressing the elephant in the room—the midlife crisis. What brings on this "crisis" and what happens at this time? While the causes and effect might differ from person to person, here are my two bits based on observations and experience.

Most of us start our forties in introspection and silence. In the inner as well as the outside world, more so within the family, there is chaos. Upheavals, actually. Just when you think that children are growing up, getting ready to take on the world, and you have been a good caretaker to your parents, your children relapse and your parents start complaining more. Just when you are coming to terms with who you are at your core, others continue to see you in the same light. And sometimes you cause that chaos—making dramatic changes to your lifestyle like solo trips, a month long stay at a Vipassana centre, loss of 30 kgs or suddenly buying a completely unnecessary summer home, so on…

Hence, the crisis. There are changes happening within you and outside of you, almost simultaneously. As you question yourself, your circumstances, and your status, the immediate world around you is doing the same. This can continue for years or even a decade or more, depending on how long you would like to extend this phase and search for answers.

I would define midlife as the time when you question everything. You look back and scrutinise what (and who) worked for you or did not. You ask what beliefs, value systems, and perceptions proved right and which ones did not. *Most importantly, you want to replace your inherited, conditioned values and beliefs with the ones that are tried and tested by you. The ones you created yourself.*

I consider the midlife crisis a *deconditioning* process—as that time when ingrained and parental or ancestral belief patterns are opened, introspected, and released if it does not feel true and acceptable to you. The "shoulds" and the "musts" are questioned to see whether you really believe in them or were indoctrinated to believe them. You look back to see if the paths you walked on were created by you or were expected from you. Every major decision—work, marriage, children, partnerships, home, finances, relationships, etc., is in the air, being juggled and reviewed closely.

Squirming under this intense scrutiny, some of those juggling balls fall from the loop. You feel the freedom of releasing this burden of incompatible beliefs yet worry about the consequences of discarding them. Hence, the crisis again.

From being a person shadowing the crowd and following the masses, you finally become an original.

If taken spiritually, this is the time your soul loudly prods and reminds you to pay heed to that inner voice, which has, so far, been silently accepting all the duties, responsibilities, and the ways of the world as a conditioned member of society. Now, the soul wants to assert itself, the reason for your birth, and see what discoveries await you in this very private, personal journey—the "I" rather than the "We".

This crisis is also created by relationships. As people prioritise themselves, they may forget to communicate this to their partners, friends, and families. Friendships/relationships may fall to the wayside as you focus on your inner growth and realise that some changes no longer resonate with your partner or a few friends.

As I realised my spiritual core and my writing need, I preferred quiet alone time which meant out of circulation with the party-going friends. Similarly, you may find that your partner of many years does not agree with your solo trips and solitary pursuits, causing friction. The shiny, sparkly new you which is slowly emerging like the proverbial caterpillar–butterfly metamorphosis, alas, cannot be reversed. It is a rather solitary journey fraught with uncertainty, yet you travel feeling confident that it will lead to a new destination.

It is with this hope that the new deconditioned you embarks, maybe creating crisis for yourself and others but replete in the belief that you deserve to live the rest of your life your own way, your most authentic way devoid of external, superficial influences. As the internal questioning lessens, the external world also settles down and what seemed like a midlife crisis welcomes the emergence of a calmer, stronger you who is eager to bestow his/her learnings on others, and in the process, conditioning them.

Oh well, such is the circle of life.

What is your eccentricity?

One of the best parts of midlife crisis is that you can blame all your eccentricities and newfound idiosyncrasies on it. Irrespective of gender, expensive "toys", cars, 6-pack abs, bikini figures, plastic surgery, sabbaticals, spiritual retreats, long drives around the country, plunges into extreme adventure—the list of indulgences is long and very personal.

My response to the crisis? Increasing passion for cars—even if I could not afford them, my attachment grew. Though this is not strictly a midlife crisis, as I have always had an almost visceral relationship with my cars.

My first memory of driving a car is not very pleasant. As an adolescent learner, I didn't know that the worst you could do was to ask your father to teach you! Sure enough, in my nervousness, I drove his car into the sidewalk, trying to avoid a large bus looming behind me. My last memory of the incident is my father torn between holding his head in exasperation and holding the wheel desperately to stabilise the car.

For many decades thereafter, I thought this ship (or rather car) had sailed.

Full disclosure—It took me till I reached forty, to get behind the wheel after this first traumatic trial. I was with a local postman who also doubled up as a car coach post his office hours. Anyway, so there I was slowly and steadily making my way at a pious 40 km/hr speed, when suddenly the infernal bus loomed up once again. This time, I was ready. I ignored the guy and peacefully continued at my steady 40 km/hr, till the bus driver lost patience and overtook me, shaking his head and probably muttering, "…these women drivers."

Today, of course, is a different story, as I zip at over 80 km/hr too. My track-weaving methods, Hindi abuses at plodding bus drivers, and horn-honking impatience fit in perfectly with the customs of quintessential Delhi drivers. The only difference is my devotion and paranoid concern for my car. So even as I weave and race away, I can proudly say that the scratches on my car have been due to the foolishness of other drivers, who cannot distinguish between a standing car and a tree!

To me, my car is less about status, comfort, transportation, etc., and more about having a living companion which is replaced only when on its last legs. The choice of car, colour, make, etc., has also mirrored my life stage and behaviour at that point in time.

The first car reflected my need for stability and the need to accommodate growing kids. It was a white, sedate hatchback—very durable and very spacious. Another full disclosure—I name all my cars, and somehow, they live up to the personality of that name. Very aptly, I named my car after a famous chariot-driven horse of a Bollywood movie—"Dhano" from the movie "Sholay". Keeping up with my sedate mindset at that time, it was a peaceful car, till severely provoked, and lasted a good, five stable years. The car proved to be a great listener to—my business strategies, values to be instilled in children, my growth in confidence and personality with the development of my professional life, etc.

Five years later—children grown up, more free time, and entry into fifties…this meant the need to prove my youthfulness and a little late rebellion—you know, all part of the midlife crisis. So came the red, jazzy sports-model, named after a fiery, hot-tempered heroine of the same Bollywood movie—"Basanti" from "Sholay", suiting the red-coloured disposition. She has been in as many escapades as her owner and mostly emerged unscathed (again, like the owner). She has patiently heard my temperamental bouts, my moments of extreme joy, and extreme despair, yet supported and facilitated my belated adventurous streak—the call for freedom and action!

Then came the time for extreme adventure—a macho, sturdy SUV called "Veeru", yes, again from "Sholay". Matching which life stage, you ask? Well, the complete denial of aging, the need to impress upon others that I have no intention of growing old gracefully and am energetic and passionate enough to put any twenty-five-year-old to shame. So, anyone in game for a long, tough drive to the mountains? Or better still, desert storming in a rugged SUV/jeep?

By the way, I am happy to join you on your midlife crisis evoked (mis)adventure! See you on the other side!

Men versus women

One last note on this topic before it is put to rest.

So, inspired by this article—*Why Midlife Crises Are Different for Women—Cleveland Clinic*—I talked to a few fellow passengers—men and women.

These were some of the differences yielded (again, at the cost of stereotyping and generalising based on a small sample… forgive me):

- Most of my male friends embraced "toys"—no, not that kind. I meant re-visiting the X-Boxes or PlayStation or flight simulators and their kind except unlike their teenage versions, these toys are now more real, with better multiverses and are far more technically superior.
- A couple of them become more serious about their hobbies, passions—creative pursuits outside of work—travelling, vlogging, six-abs, etc.
- Thankfully, a few realised their burgeoning abdomen and become sportier—going back to their youthful zests—football, cricket, tennis, squash, etc.
- And yes I knew one or two who decided to experiment outside their marriage, too private to tell…ahem, *cough, cough*.

As the article states, men may tend to seek escape from the looping trap of daily life that has dogged at their heels for decades.

Now women? They go through many more internal and external changes, hence their reactions may be a tad different. While men may seek external stimulation or escape tactics, women tend to become more introspective and self-focused. Again, generalising, women who have so far been care-givers to family members, children, etc., now realise that they have been neglecting themselves. So, their list….

- Need for more socialising and female companionship, particularly when travelling or just indulging in fun activities. I still long to create an all-middle-aged female bowling troop. Any takers?
- More awareness about health, hormones, exercise, and well-being. We cleverly discuss each other's problems with our gynaecologists to ensure varied opinions and then discuss them over numerous glasses of wine
- A few decide why not start smoking, wining, and the myriad of anxiety-reducing vices. No judgements. Escape is important for women too.
- More creative routes also brought into focus again alongside more reading, more travelling, etc.
- Many hours spent examining the new lines on the face, skin drooping around the mouth, and hot debates around Botox, anti-ageing processes, fat suction methods and so on. My stance? Do not grow gracefully and if you have the money, flaunt it on your face and hair

Facetiousness apart, the common thread in both the lists is re-discovery; however, the expression differs. While men may need more physically-involving activities, women may seek fewer demanding routes and maybe, even more insular ones.

I am all for relentless rediscoveries, anything to avoid ennui and enervation; version 2.0 has just begun.

4

Changing Relationships with Work, Money, and You

GENTLY propelled by an unseeing force—I suspect your evolving core—things unravel a bit. The first victims of this collateral damage? Mostly, they are the ones that eat up most of your time—money, ways of work, business. Work and money get examined the most, tossed and turned to see if any stones have been left unturned. As you look deep within, a few disappointments, lessons, and insights are revealed, which form your new attitude towards work, money, and most importantly, about your own personality.

Uncovering "Multi-potentialities"

Ever since the conundrum of middle-life crisis hit, somewhat discomfited, I have tried multiple novel activities, learnt a few new skills, and stuck with a subset of those. Perhaps this strikes a similar chord with some of you?

A few of these interests continued. However, I was not passionate enough to make them public or make a career out of them *as yet*. Am I good at them? Yes, sure. Am I an expert in them? Not really, I don't think so because that would mean I have mastered them, which I haven't and neither would I want to, as that would mean the end of learning.

Yet for other things tried, once I understood what they entailed, I could not muster enough enthusiasm to get further ingrained into them, nor did they stay. Maybe these were fly-by-night operators, ships that pass in the night, etc.

Maybe I just did not care enough to put the hard work needed to fructify the interest. *And that gave me the answer I needed. I really did not care enough to make something more out of them.* Rather than feeling guilty, I turned to the guru Google and found a quiz that somewhat explains who I always was and have further fossilised into. Wait for it... drumroll... *I am a mixed style multi-potentialist.*

What??? I know, I know, let me explain.

"Mixed style multi-potentialities people just like to mix up things and work. They are...

- *Happiest when they have a mix of few different projects on their plate at any given time.*
- *Love variety but get overwhelmed when they have too much.*
- *Sometimes go through periods where they are juggling a bunch of different projects and, also, periods where they are deeply invested in a single thing."*

(https://puttylike.com)

I could relate to this so much and was so relieved to understand it. I was always an avidly curious human being, but the middle-ages have translated this into the complete inability to do only one thing at a time.

One of the things that a multi-potential person should understand is that he/she indulges in juggling multiple interests, learnings, and vocations for the sheer experience and knowledge provided, and not because there is an earth-shattering need to use them or earn from them. It is done just for the heck of it, to fulfil some seeking need within, and hence, once it is known and revealed, it is over and done with. No need to feel guilty or unhappy about not making something substantive. It just existed for as long as there was a curiosity about it.

I am sure there are many of us out there who feel that living is more than just our immediate job, surroundings, and circumstances. Those of us who admire what others know and are doing, want to do it too, and are constantly trying new things as novelty fulfils their restless streak. For a few of us, this need to experiment becomes more pronounced as we grow, maybe due to a growing awareness that the body is slowing down a little, so fill up the days with as much learning as possible.

In my defence, all I can say is that the more we learn about ourselves, the more we learn about the world around us.

The era of career transitions

In the process of ripping off the metaphorical band aid, your work sphere gnaws at the fabric of your being. In all likelihood, fed up with the demands of employment or the banality of it all, we start contemplating and even jumping into entrepreneurship, all the way or part of the way.

Having done both—tried to be an entrepreneur a few times and worked with one over several occasions, here are some helpful tips even as you submit to its lure:

- As entrepreneurs, we are like kids who have a new toy—we want everyone to see it and play with it, yet we know it is ours. This shiny and intriguing piece of our life that only we can own. That is the baser instinct, no matter how well shrouded it is in the veneer of delegation.
- At one point or the other, just as you share your children with the outside world, you will also have to share your business with others—employees, clients or customers, and stakeholders. See if you can differentiate between passion and control.
- Do not expand or try to become more than a sole proprietor if you can't share your venture with others. It's fine to remain a one-man show and restrict it to what you can manage single-handedly. But the minute you are ambitious and want to create a company or an organisation, you will have to let go and allow the baby to grow from toddler to a child to an adult. That means there will be influences that are not yours in the business.
- If you have the skills, competence, and courage to go solo, do so by all means. Yet, I repeat, always remember your motivations for going solo and do not become overly ambitious unless you are willing to re-enter the cycle of working with and for others, including feedback, etc.

- Entrepreneurs can also become narcissistic and may be tempted to reward sycophants. Again, it is important to disassociate ego from your creation, your venture, and decide what parts you want to control and what you don't.
- As an entrepreneur, you hire talent that can take the load off your shoulders, yet you can become insecure when they connect with the audience, client, or customers that you have so painfully assimilated. Again, let go.
- The ultimate success of an entrepreneur is not that he/she has created something successful, but that he/she has allowed it to grow in order for it to be a success.

Now that you have assimilated all of the above, go forth and set sail. Your entrepreneurial boat and sea of vast opportunities await.

Under scrutiny—the employed

On the heels of entrepreneurship is the other side of the coin—employment, another area scrutinised and introspected intensely after almost 25–30 years devoted to it. You become painfully aware that there is a mistiness hanging over your employed life, it does seem to have slowed to a Victorian pace in the 21st century momentum you are surrounded in.

I remember sulking for hours about my full-time, 9-to-5 job, lamenting. Had it not been for the compulsive need for financial stability, the predictability of income, would I even be in this job? And so began the intense scrutiny, as I put my job under a magnified microscope observing closely how it squirmed like an overheated worm.

As I parted the cells and atoms of my job, I remembered a discussion with a CXO-level friend. She was grumbling how her entrepreneurial husband would react every time she wanted to bow out of her steady and high paycheck. Before the grievances could spiral out of control, we jumped to a more amusing comparison between marriage and employment. Many similarities immediately came to mind...

- Both marriage and jobs give security and stability.
- Both may become routine after some years.
- Both tend to become habits.
- Both can herald conflicting emotions—one day you love them, another day you get angry, yet another day you may just about tolerate them, and in your good days, you may get peace from them.
- Both can become predictable.
- Both take a lot of time and energy to sustain and can be fairly demanding on some occasions.
- Both may come with a sense of loss of freedom (not many will own to that!)

After a hearty laugh, we also realised that there are thankfully some differences too that possibly places marriage above employment. Your spouse of many years will understand and respond to you... there is a flexibility in the relationship that allows the marriage to change with changing times.

On the other hand, office jobs with their rules, processes, or structures may create a rigidity, robbing people of joy and creativity. There is little flexibility to experiment, and outcomes become the driving principle. Marriage is largely between two individuals, though witnessed by a few close family members. However, offices/jobs are surrounded by many who are scrutinising, weighing, judging, and deciding for you.

The need to showcase quantitative outcomes obliterate the beauty of qualitative outcomes in jobs. Marriage is still held together with the qualitative aspects of time, effort, and emotion "invested". Wouldn't it be great if work institutions can start resembling happy marriages?

Having reached that happy conclusion, we continued to enjoy our bitching session. Don't begrudge us this relieving pleasure, it's like that joke you know—a soldier winces and groans as he puts on his tight fitted hard boots. A fellow soldier asks him, "Why don't you ask for a better fitting pair?" "What?! And remove the only pleasure I get in my day, the ecstatic relief when I remove them!" was the soldier's response.

How do we win in this technological "race"

Remember that fable, the race between the hare and the tortoise? Well, the younger generations are the hares and we are the tortoises, generally speaking. But hey, remember who won the race, right?!

Here is another unravelling, let's face it—we are being challenged at both the workplace and at home from the tech-savvy youth and by our own minds. Our authority and supremacy over our own neat little world comes to a resounding halt as we realise we are being left behind in this galloping race of technological advancements.

Do we compete with the speed and fast grasp of the youth? Do we rise and not join the race at all? Should we become guides and mentors? Or should we wing it and learn to compete, and then pass on the baton as in a relay race? As we question ourselves in the face of an increasingly unfamiliar outside world, the one thing that we really need to do is slow down. We need to pause, reflect, and maybe even take a sabbatical (now I understand why householders in ancient times took off to the jungles).

This slowing down makes us think laterally, how we add meaning now to others and the self, and thereby "win" the race of needing to be useful when technology becomes a mire.

Let's just become the wise tortoise when the hares run out of steam!

When I am talking of a race, I don't mean acquisitions, materialistic pursuits, or promotions, though those can also be your goalposts. To each his or her own. I mean the race to be useful, to still matter, to be a voice that others still want to hear and not disappear into oblivion. This definition of race is a very inherent part of human existence, the call of our ego that just does not fade away.

At the end of the day, we all want to be perceived as being useful. In this race of recognition of our relevance, we do not want our family members or our community to forget us. Often these feelings come because we wonder about our usefulness.

Mostly, we resurrect parts of us that fill the gap left by a scrambling climb to a whimsical top. We realise that slowing down will mean a faster pace to new, maybe even loftier, goals and we can then race ahead towards our new quests.

When you get pink-slipped

Almost as a side effect to being employed is the alarmingly rising phenomenon of being "laid off", terminated, or other similar semantics. Long story short, you have been pink-slipped (I do not like the colour associated with this extremely unloving act—why not call it the black slip, just sayin').

The signs keep building up… business is badly down, the economy is suffering, companies are not investing, clients are not spending, and the excel sheets are in the red.

"Bosses"—I have never liked the word, and now less so, as it implies a superiority that is not always the case—start dropping broad hints and gentle warnings couple of months before the D-day. Now the hopeless optimist in us says, "Yes, things are bad right now, but it will become better. No way but the way up, blah blah." The higher-ups largely remain unconvinced, shaking their heads and making dark and pessimistic predictions of how things will not look up. Sheesh, it feels like battle lines have been drawn, and *we are living in dark times, Harry Potter!* All of this under the guise of: "We are being realistic."

So back to work it was, following the adage "do your work sincerely and the fruits of your labour will surely follow." You ensure the team is motivated and there is bonhomie between them and other units. Next, meet clients to the extent they would want to meet, write thoughtful and strategic proposals, do not leave a single pitch unanswered, and ensure the team receives their due and promotions. After all, you have to put your best foot forward.

But the stubborn numbers refuse to move by the leaps and bounds the senior leadership wants. They want floods in a drought situation and the numbers grow painfully by bits and pieces. Targets are being dictated by the mystical, secretive, "big-brother-is-watching-you" kind of board of stakeholders at headquarters. When all else fails, the blame is put on this ubiquitous entity that no one has ever seen or talked to, but that watches you behind the curtains…brrrr…creepy.

One fine day, the "superior" shows up looking dark and ominous, and bites out tensely, "Can we talk?" Uh oh, the precursor to every divorce or argument. So, in you go to a cabin far away from the madding crowd, and the superior starts. "I don't know how to say this, so will come straight to the point. You have been asked to leave."

"Ha, so now you are being truthful when all along you were feeding lies," is the first thought that comes. You are shocked but also deep down expecting this, after all the atmosphere in the office with everyone shutting each other out through headphones, staring diligently at the screen, and talking serious stuff on the phone, speak eloquently of the fear of being fired. You listen numbly, uncomprehendingly to the convoluted explanations, catching words and phrases disjointedly, "stakeholders", "business numbers", "recession", "poor economy", "I tried my best to fight back", "the senior leadership demanded cut in salary costs", etc.

Your only overwhelming thought is, "How on earth can my measly salary make such a dent in your profits?"

And then the guilt-struck boss continues, "You are not the only one, many other senior heads will also roll (though not his own!)… this is not a reflection of your abilities or performance, you should not let this undermine your confidence, blah blah blah."

"Ok, now wait just a **##@@** minute. Of course, this job is not a reflection of my abilities or intelligence, as I know what my true potential is." You tell yourself indignantly. And that's when you say to hell with dignity and ask some pointed, impolite questions, such as, "When business picks up, who will do the work? When you don't have a senior business development person, how will the business come? The economy, world, business will go through cyclical ups and downs, so will you keep hiring and firing? If I am so clever and talented, why are you not investing in me and committing to me the way I invested my time and energy in your company? How can I alone be held responsible for a struggling business when all you higher-ups are supposed to be the heads?"

All very valid questions met with stoic silence and a pitying look that says, "I understand you are in pain and are venting."

And then enters the grand old dame—the senior HR lady, who till today did not know of your existence or name. She starts with, "Sorry, how sad it is to meet for the first time in sad circumstances." Hey, stop treating it like a tragedy. That is supposed to be my stance. Don't take this last pleasure away from me.

So long story short, look for another job. Sure, it will come, but this time you know to commit to yourself and the work first, and then the place.

Money and the middle-aged—mirroring the journey

On the footsteps of work follows its major benefit—money.

Now money and some of us middle-aged have a strange relationship. Sometimes, it is a profoundly serious, deeply committed marriage of two kindred souls. Other times, we are like boxers at opposite ends of the boxing ring, circling each other warily for the next move. In a more balanced time, we are friends looking after each other, yet not intensely involved.

By this time in life, we have spent many decades together. Our relationship started in our early twenties, and by now we usually form a sort of mutual understanding. At first, we were like wary acquaintances, there was a curiosity to know each other and explore common points and kindred interests. At times, money had the upper hand and at other times we did. We gave our ego, credentials, and passions a lot more importance, but money did follow like a faithful companion, mirroring the efforts. It grew as we grew, even lauded our efforts and hard work by jumping ahead.

Our relationship was fluid, free flowing, which really meant neither did we have any control over it, nor did money have a control over our actions. Yet there was this reciprocity, and so long as confidence kept it boosted, money grew. We were loyal and faithful like partners who were in for the long haul.

Closer to the middle-ages, there are disturbances—the entry of the "other" in our blossoming relationship, and a phenomenon that happens to the best of us—stagnancy or a plateauing effect. With this doomed flatness came the accompaniments—disappointment, self-doubt, crushed ego, etc. You get the drift. And poof goes money. It warily watches us from far away, wanting no part in this debacle. Suddenly, it moves from the status of a loyal partner to a flirtatious mistress looking for the next excitement of growth, possibly even seeking younger shores. You plead, beg, entice, and give guarantees, but it takes time to get convinced, and we enter the boxing ring.

So, you change tracks. You stop begging for its mercy, and instead started commanding it, controlling it, and pushing it into a forced partnership, victorious in the slinging match. Depending on the force used, money stays steady, slowly responding, yet not bounding ahead or leaping forth as it used to. Like an old worn-out couple, we stay committed to each other, but the joy of togetherness is missing. And you realise once more in this tumultuous journey with money that the force-fit hadn't really worked. We were together yet were neither soulmates nor friends.

Wisdom prevails, so you let in some air, freshness, and breathing space. Letting go of unreal, youthful expectations and fearful restrictions, you loosen the stranglehold and let the free flow happen once again. Showing deep respect, you invite money to the doorstep, but let it cross the threshold only if it wants to. You start making decisions independently, all the while keeping the door open, knowing that curiosity and adventure would keep money nearby. It peeks into the room, sniffs the whiff of hope, shivers excitedly at the newness of fresh thinking, and absorbs the sun's rays around. It watches, voluntarily arrested by the pace of developments but content to be an avid observer.

Do not lose patience, or gnash teeth in frustration or browbeat the fellow into submission. Hang on to the last rope of tolerance. Continue what you are now a pro at—experiences unmindful of success or failure, making a few twists and turns and fresh starts along the way, determined not to be in any battle with money. We could be friendly acquaintances if not best friends.

Suffice it to say, the middle-aged partnership is still continuing. Tentatively, we have mutually decided to give each other space and not intrude into the other's territory. So, money blooms where it sees guarantees and stays friends where it sees risks and unpredictability. In that balanced relationship, we can hopefully now stay for decades, both of us happy in this unconventional live-in relationship. Parts of us are committed to each other and parts of us flow to greener pastures.

For we have cracked the formula—where love flows, money follows.

5

Your Middle-Aged Body

One of the biggest clues to the middle-ages lies in the body's dismantling bits. Along with everything else, this too demands the attention and review of the middle-aged, insistently so. What happens, how do we deal with it…now that's a mystery waiting to be solved.

Like money, food too is a journey still unravelling

Aaahh, the days when we could drool over food, eat anything that looked good and tasted better. The days when any amount of sugar, fat, or carbs could enter our stomach without repercussions. The days when chocolate, french fries, and pizzas were a part of everyday life… one does miss those days.

Now, every calorie is counted and every label is scrutinised for nutritional status and content. What looks good is discarded for what is good for the stomach, and green is the only colour that dominates the plate. Indulgence with sugar and oils is kept for special occasions and bad moods.

It just takes a little time for the mind to catch up with the body—to look at food in a certain way and make that green salad, that sugar free cake, that dark chocolate a little more palatable. Do not give up, it can happen. It helps to stay clear of your children and not share meals with them and definitely not pick sundry delicious bits from their plates. There is a limit to how much cruelty one can impose on the hapless brain that is still trying to come to terms with the middle-aged stomach.

Frequent trips to the dietician, nutritionist, dermatologist, and friends who positively gloat about their healthy and green living become a must. Sitting with great envy, and yes, great boredom while peers go on about their new ultra-green lifestyles. You drift off as the ever-fertile imagination draws up visions of melting, gooey, moist chocolate brownies and ice cream. Eyes glaze over as you enthusiastically chomp the leaves on the plate, forcibly visualising them as green-coloured doughnuts. It is almost like no part of us—eyes, tongue, or mind want to accept this new reality.

So, like our relationship with money, we create a new relationship with food—an uneasy truce. Feed the body well most days and allow moments of indulgence. Avoid pictures of slim, younger you in your heydays, and rely on clothes that flatter you without revealing the layers and girths. As we make peace with our new shape and the vulnerabilities of the much-tortured stomach, you feel free to find somewhat tasty, healthy food—yes, that oxymoron can be found.

You see, after much experimentation with a multitude of diets, failed follow-ups on advice, intermittent fasting, etc., there is finally a reliable formula—listen to your body. Seriously, that's all it took—freedom to express and awareness to listen to it.

Your stomach and body are teaching you on a daily basis what they respond well to and what they do not. So, pay heed and feed the stomach what it wants, the only compromise being that the unhealthy, tasty foods were reduced to mere morsels and titbits, but not completely denied. Healthy foods could be eaten watching or reading something entertaining, so they feel better too, and small portions become the only mantra to be followed. Water becomes the new nectar and stomach filler.

Today we stand heroic and proud of all of these relationships—with money, work, food—well, most of the relationships; still have to figure out the ones with fellow human beings.

An understanding journey: Body and I

Early morning walks *groan*, that is definitely not what makes me get up every morning. It's more like my filter coffee—if anyone comes between me and my cuppa, I am like a disgruntled mama bear. What I do feel very grateful for, is my hard-working body that continues on its auto mode as if instructed not by us but by a divine order of things.

Now here is the catch at the middle-ages—we cannot take our body for granted, ill-treat it, burden it with emotional stresses and hormonal imbalances, well, it will protest more than it will crusade.

No one knows of this protest more than my dear male friend who continued on his dune-bashing, heroic rescues of stranded ignorant tourists, oblivious to the deceptive softness of the tall dunes till one fine day it crashed. Literally.

On one of his dunes bashing trips, driving at high velocity to climb the formidable dunes, the hard rock hidden under the sands was not visible leading the car to ram into it at high speed, flying several feet in the air. The landing was not soft on his middle-aged body nor his beloved rugged jeep. Several days at the hospital, physiotherapy sessions, and pumped with medicines, his body said, "Mate, this is it. Slow down or I will make you." Not an empty threat. He is still recovering six months later and now, respects his sandy trips and the dunes more. Not that he has stopped, just slowed down.

As middle-ages approach and show us how we have treated this beautifully complex yet balanced frame of ours, maybe it's time to bow our heads in shame and fold our hands in gratitude. We make a pact—"I will try my best not to overwhelm you with things that are unnecessary and not worthy of your effort. And, I will also try to treat you with the respect you deserve and give you what you ask. At the very least, I will try to listen to what we both need."

As the body gives in gracefully to the process of living, aging, and experiencing, it asks us to be cognizant of this process, asks us to clear space so it can be light and stay light. It needs to continue functioning efficiently, but now, in its halftime of the game of life, a little reverse care is also needed. The body now faces its biggest challenge—sustaining us as we reinvent ourselves for the adventures beyond midlife.

Body and I, part II: The dichotomy

Even as we make compromises with our middle-aged bodies, there is another battle brewing—a dichotomous pull and push between the body and the mind. Or, to be more exact, there is actually a pull and push from the mind, but the body is inclined to do neither. It just wants to stay in an inert position of rest. Of course, it may still be forced out of its lethargy through sheer will-power—again a powerful boost from the mind.

This truly is the biggest realisation that we struggle with. The heart is still young and seeking adventures, but the poor body is recouping from all the arduous hardships enforced on it from the early years. The wear and tear, leakages (metamorphically and literally), and the spasms of weakening muscles are real. So the body, rather than blindly following the behest of the mind as it has done in the past, is now in strike mode.

As usual, the restless mind and the adventurous emotional reaction of the heart send a signal to the resting legs. The legs stay wooden, as if nailed to the couch and send back the signal unequivocally, "No!" The mind and heart, confused, call a hurried counsel, "There is zero cooperation, what do we do now?" Crossed legs, with arms also crossed behind head, the leisurely body yawns, amusedly watching the flurry of confused thoughts.

Soon, a verdict is reached, "Forget it. Let's just distract ourselves with some nice shows, drinks, and foods." And that's that. The body celebrates and burrows deeper inside the cover. Yet the mind and the heart, though in a temporary truce with the body, are vaguely dissatisfied. Whether that thought, feeling, and instinct was correct or not can only be ratified by action, which the body has rejected, so it plagues them like an unsolved puzzle.

To do or not to do is the dilemma for the body as it follows the path of least resistance and chooses the easy, lazy way out, burdened by the heavy lunch, burgeoning waist lines, and a general sense of wellbeing. The mind races on, oblivious to the slowdown of these middle-ages, and loses a lot of energy in its rush to reach nowhere. The heart decides it seems to be the sanest and most balanced of the lot, so carefully sifts through the thoughts of the mind and gently persuades the body when it *feels* that action is now imperative and useful.

And so, we end up moving and doing what *feels* right rather than what is thought of as right. Now, if only exercise was something that felt right too!

When menopause and other "female" problems hit

As a middle-aged woman who has undergone menopause, I will not be able to do justice to my peers if I do not write about the earth-shattering phenomenon of this age group.

I have read vague smatterings of how menopause and puberty also affect men, but since the evidence of this remains a little intangible, it is assumed that menopause, in the traditional sense, is a woman's experience, just as menstruation is.

I am not sure if men are sensitised to menopause and I suspect it is not very well understood by women either, till it hits you. However, it is a very gnawing issue for middle-aged women—pre and post menopause. After you undergo it for some time, you can find the humorous side in between the hot flashes, bursts of red-hot irritation, and the general feeling that you have ballooned thrice your normal size.

Middle-aged women are ill prepared for menopause, and it takes many trips to the gynaecologist and late-night conversations with fellow passengers to realise that this is a force to be reckoned with. Diets, exercises, etc., seem to be too mild to handle the burgeoning stomach layer. Days start lethargically and stay in a state of inertia. The tiniest of triggers set off alarm systems which in turn create outbursts. The mirror becomes your enemy and food dishes are approached with suspicion, which really does not help, as rampant mood swings make you want to attack that chocolate bar with great gusto.

"Exercise, exercise," screams the mind, "sleep, sleep," begs the body, and the poor, silent heart just wants a break. Everything slows down, along with most of your memory, and it is nerve-racking to recollect what you wanted to say seconds ago. Midway through your official Zoom meeting, you suddenly remember that important bill you haven't paid, and absent-mindedness is as routine as brushing teeth.

You sweat in the iciest of AC temperatures, even as the aches in your wrists and joints remind you that you are freezing under the icy blast. All you want is to be left alone, yet melancholy settles in if ignored even for an hour. And do not even get me started on how alien and irritating some body parts feel. Your erstwhile glowing face and skin starts to dull, and you develop a sudden interest in cosmetic treatments, plastic surgery, and anti-aging processes. "Hormonal imbalances" becomes the most used Google search keyword and you wish you had paid more attention to your yoga and meditation classes.

The only silver lining, if one at all, is that hot-tempered menopause substitutes the annoying monthly menstrual cycles—what a bouquet of choices for women! Never mind, I am just feeling grumpy—menopaused, you know. But seriously, men and family members, do look after and look deeper at the middle-aged women in your midst—their suffering may seem silent, but there is a lot of internal chaos happening. I have seriously started looking for places of cool climate the whole year round, my friends are seriously contemplating buying boxing punching bags and yet others are searching for mobile, small air conditioners.

My next book may be dedicated to menopause, it honestly deserves a lot of written real estate.

6

Your Middle-Aged Mind

THE body has been understood, new relations have been formed with work and money, and it's all under control, right? Kind of…there are still some more aftermaths of middle-ages to be dealt with to emerge victorious. This is the time when comforting lassitude has to be fought, a foggy memory starts to make its presence felt, the greys and silvers are more than just a lining, and social media keeps you on its toes.

The frenemy

After that overload, let's move to easier pastures. So, how was the Netflix bingeing? And how was that favourite corner of the sofa—you know, the one spot that carries a permanent imprint of your posterior? And what about those packs of (hopefully oil free, sugar free, sodium free, trans fats free, and God knows what all else free of) snacks? Calm down, I am not taking you on a guilt trip. I understand, we really have hit midlife and drooping down is a side effect. In fact, it even closely resembles a reward for all those decades of toil.

And that is the difference between the lassitude of yesteryears and the middle-aged. We start *justifying* our lethargy and sort of feel like we deserve it.

After that bout of sympathy, let's get a little real, shall we? Long spells of lethargy, while very relaxing and gratifying, can lead to some addictive laziness. Midlife also does come with lowering physical stamina and activity level amongst many of us who have not been regularly exercising. I am not talking about those athletic determined midlife travellers who seem to have limitless energy and stamina for really mind-boggling long marathons. Just seeing their self-congratulatory posts and videos makes me tired. Let me stop rambling and come back to the point about us lethargic beings—while lethargy might be a real issue, the bigger problem is laziness.

I define laziness as a frenemy of the middle-aged. It coaxes us into never ending relaxation, hypnotising us with its logic of self-indulgence. We justify its insidious hold over us with many rationales till it becomes a part of us—a habit. Once that happens, let's just say, it is the beginning of the end. The end of instant pick-me-up, spontaneity, get up and go, and all those zestful proactive states of being. You think, you wonder, you weigh to see whether that action is more necessary than laziness and if not, aah the sofa beckons. This state is particularly pronounced during the weekends and any outside visits evoke a protesting groan.

You become more selective, more realistic about what you can and cannot do, and the day really cannot have more than one agenda. In short, laziness wins and drooping seems easier than straightening. I understand. I am just about dropping off writing this piece… *yawn*… more later….

Brain fog

On the heels of an increasingly addled existence comes the brain fog…

As the pen hovers over the paper, the brain struggles to remember what it was going to write.

Welcome to the middle-age induced brain fog which I politely call "preoccupation". This is a state of many insignificant moments lost to an overburdened mind. Blame it on the 30 years of working life, or the travails of raising children, or the dismal state of world affairs, etc., but definitely don't blame it on the 50 odd years of existence!

Ok, now that was a blatant untruth—the fact of the matter is that there is sometimes a hazy fog of forgetfulness hanging like a cloud around the middle-aged brain. So, there are a series of hilarious (for other family members) happenings as a result….

- The most common—you enter a room, exit, re-enter—all the while wondering what exactly made you enter the room in the first place.
- Clutching tightly the mobile phone, you call and scream blue murder on those who had last handled it demanding it be found immediately.
- You send the weighing machine for repairs—of course you have forgotten your last month's weight, the machine is berserk and is pulling out crazy double digits.
- All your passwords are the same across devices, ATM, debit, and credit cards—at least it is not 1234. You curse every time the software update demands you to change the password for your own security, what if you forget.

- You repeat the same vitamin pill same day—who remembers the last time you had it.
- The car keys have to be in the same bunch as the house and office keys—it's just easier to carry even if it means stranded house members waiting for your return.
- Reminders across devices and a mega one on the fridge to remind you to look at the reminders.
- Working and communication hours shrink—11 a.m. to 5 p.m.—high levels of irritability for calls thereafter.
- Punctuality follows the law of diminishing returns—your return to it is diminishing.
- Comfortable clothes is the need of the hour, the fact that it hides the burgeoning belly is just a coincidence.
- Last and not the least—there are reading glasses, short distance ones, long distance glasses, sunglasses, and most importantly a chain around the neck to keep track of all of them. Yes, we have tried the photochromatic ones too

I know, a lot of exaggeration there but just wanted to make sure you know what we go through.

Easing into social media

There is one space where the brain fog increases even more—social media. My forays with the social media have become increasingly sparse and sporadic. In the early years, these platforms reached a crescendo along with watching Netflix, etc., till the feeds, posts, stories, reels and so on became too many to keep track of. I turn to my children and youngsters for advice on handling this barrage of junk.

And then there was those "warnings" of data security and privacy penetrating through my firewall of naivete. Moreover, the ten thousand ways of blemishing hair style, the wonder creams, and serums promising that all the 50+ years' worth of wrinkles and scars would fade into oblivion, well, just seemed belittling. How do you assume that we would be ashamed of our appearance, or the wear and tear of a life well-spent and still be rolling with the punches.

Fed up with the "targeted" ads and stories—less of "social" and more of "marketing"—I exit, better to go back to the original ways of socialising—meetings, calls, parties, get-togethers. But wait, all my friends want selfies during parties. Damn, is there no way out!

Oh, by the way, have you subscribed to my YouTube channel?! Blasted social media, what can I say—can't live with it, can't live without it.

Salt and pepper

Famous words by the famed Hollywood actor Morgan Freeman:

Funny thing about getting older: your eyesight starts getting weaker but your ability to see through people's bullshit gets much better.

Sure, agreed wholeheartedly. After all, life is a huge teacher. The shades of salt and pepper in you—lingering naivety and hard-earned discernment—do become an advantage if balanced.

But that's not the salt and pepper that I want to talk about. No such prosaic thoughts. Right now, there is a bigger, more immediate debate at hand—to retain the salt and pepper, to wholly salt it, or to pepper it completely? What am I talking about? The hair, of course.

I do notice many women around me who have just shaken off this social obligation and gone completely grey. Men, of course seem to debate less around the issue, they draw even more admiration towards their greying temples—claimed symbols of intellect and wisdom. Younger women seem to like that about them. On the other hand, greying women seem to get cast away as old and so we turn to dear old L'oreal to intensify the pepper and keep up the charade of looking decades younger.

My compromise? I promise to turn myself in and embrace "greyhood" once the wrinkles start appearing. Till then, I pour pepper all over the emerging greys.

7

Friendships–The Bright Side

AMIDST all these tumbling and turning, there is one real silver stable lining. We rediscover friends. They come back or we go back to them, happy that there are those who still know us, who have been with us and are on the same path. Equally happy to discover new ones on the same journey.

Aaahhh—friendships

Caught in the throes of working life, raising children, meeting spouse and parent needs, maintaining the home, etc., this is the one part of our life that we mostly neglect.

It takes long gaps and crisis moments to realise that sometimes the immediate and extended family is not enough. The empathy of friends travelling the same travesties as you, undergoing the same transformative decade, is just not to be found elsewhere. They understand your life stage immediately.

Friends know why bars and pubs are your favourite hangout zone, after all, they accompany you there. Friends know why you whisper your sorrows from the bathroom at 2 a.m., as they are listening to you from their own. Friends understand why you cannot talk to your spouse, grown-up children, or aging parents—let's face it, sometimes they are the issue!

I lament the loss of friends the most, and I am deeply intrigued and morbidly fascinated by individuals who get by without friends for long stretches of time or have just one or two. I confess, I need deep meaningful regular conversations with the fellow middle-aged to survive, and genuinely fail to understand how we can get by without it. Men too are quick to admit the need for significant friendships and run to sports bars, gyms, or just about anywhere they can have some leg-pulling or heavy discussions around money, business, sports, politics, and so on. Its contribution to physical health in the middle-ages is a known fact.

There are also many men who know how to be platonic friends with women, and they will swear by their contribution. The vice versa also holds true.

I dare say, however, that I have added nuances to my middle-aged friendships. I have become more selective, more balanced, and need reciprocal ones. It seems enough for me and from what I hear, for others too, to cultivate the more qualitatively superior friendships. By now, it is expected that you will not be that narcissistic and self-absorbed friend of your younger years and are not seeking friendships to purge your sorrows and worries, but to share and care. So, I retain those that offer the fresh oxygen of unselfish friendships. You know, the ones that are not defined by your social stature or net worth, but by the warmth of your heart.

My near and dear friends and I agree that we need not become too selective. In fact, there is a conscious effort to make new friends, join like-minded people with similar interests, look for company at hobby classes and meetups. One of my closest friends was my client, thankfully we didn't work together so, could build a lasting relationship.

Again, not to say that we do not have younger friends, we do. They are great to party with, to go on long treks and do all those physically-demanding activities that make us proud when we can walk in step with them. But we come back to our college friends, school friends, similar aged friends for comfort like warm blankets that you never tire of. They listen carefully, flinch emotionally when you break down, smile at your follies, and expressively abuse you if you neglect or let them down. They just know and that is what makes them feel more familiar than the very entertaining younger friends.

Of womance and bromance

Interestingly, I had to look up the female equivalent of bromance, and "womance" came up as the answer. The fact that the computer's dictionary does not recognise it further reiterates the lack of attention given to this phenomenon.

Women are the hidden yet natural leaders in the family—whether or not it is proven, and whether or not we agree to it. She decides the tenor of daily life, she inspires. She also provides the resources, financial and otherwise, and she creates the hearth and the home.

So where does the middle-aged woman of the house go when she needs support? It may be provided by the partner/spouse, children, or rest of her family members, but more often than not, this is a best-case scenario. As she looks around her, suddenly she notices she has been left alone. Busy taking care of her work, children, home, food, husband, etc., she doesn't notice when the children grow old and fly away from the nest or when the husband has become set in his ways. Or if she is a single mom, then, well, she has been left alone.

As empty nesters or even amongst those without children, we want to rekindle our womances, trying to resurrect old friendships and find new ones. As one of the early birds in this realisation, it came as a bit of a setback that commonalities had whittled away. At the risk of generalising, women do tend to be more home focused. Hobbies, entertainment, and travel are all things she may have planned for but have not taken off as yet. For a few, she may also need the right company. For the lucky ones, the extended family can provide womance, while for others, some searching, joining clubs, and hobby-based meetups may be needed.

As a remote worker and a single mother, I had the privilege of staying with my working son and college-going daughter at the United States for extended time periods. Very soon, however, I realised that they did not have time to socialise with me and I was bored of waiting. I decided, I must make new friends even if I knew no one in Chicago.

I joined an organisation I had heard of some time back—InterNations—a global platform that brings expats together, spread across 166 countries. I made a few connects before I went for the first event—a Salsa dance lesson and party! Riding on a wave of bravado, I joined some 20 odd people, happy that all of them looked equally lost. Had it not been for a wonderful host who ensured everyone was introduced and greeted, it would have been a flop show.

After several trips and even more events, I am proud to know closely a few from Venezuela, Korea, Brazil, Lebanon, and Italy who stay connected whether I am in Chicago or not. Their stories, cultural backdrop, family sagas, and issues make me realise how truly similar our lives are and how warm human connections can be if we were to just stay open.

Whether it is womance or bromance, the middle-ages is a time when we rediscover friendships beyond the tight circle of a couple of close friends. Some are successful, and we rediscover the joys of friendships, while for others, the choice of making new friends at a late age seems a formidable challenge. The more flexible you are in terms of cultural backgrounds, age, education, etc., the higher the chances of increasing your circle. Though this applies across ages, it becomes particularly important for the middle-aged before they become too selective.

Of nostalgia and reunions

When thinking of friendships, it is inevitable that you will travel back to your early ones—those formed in school, college, and early workplaces. Remember those times when the world was a colourful rainbow, when furtive drinking, smoking, parties, and gossip about each other ruled the days? Sigh… where did those days go?

Cleaning out closets and chests of drawers lead to the discovery of old photos and memories hitting fast and furious. Innocence blazed amidst the joy of tender years—some of those friends stayed, some drifted away, and yet others moved away deliberately. Some still care and call, some exchange intermittent WhatsApp's, and many stay silent and distant. Interesting, right?

Missing that naïve spontaneity, lack of status, judgments, and high level of inclusion, we yearn for the hues of innocent younger days.

Then it is decided, how about a reunion? Splendid idea! After many months of checking schedules, obtaining RSVPs, coordinating, and booking venues, exhausted, we wait for the D-day. Nervousness increases steadily and thoughts hit fast and furious. "Have I gained too much weight? Is my bald patch showing? Or worse, am I balder than others? What should I wear to hide the creeping tyres? Are spouses invited? Should he/she come? What will they think about me?" and so on....

Taking a deep breath and doing some last-minute crash diets and glam shopping, you take that final step towards attending the reunion.

Surprisingly, it is easy and smooth. You realise most are dealing with the same health, wealth, job, and children's issues as you. Most have also gained varying degrees of weight, experienced baldness, and very few have grown old gracefully. Of course, it helps those draining topics like politics and current affairs get substituted in the nostalgia of cherished togetherness—teachers, college trips, and events. Couples who were together at college now acknowledge each other awkwardly or laugh sheepishly at their follies.

Swept in the moment, together we look back tenderly at our younger selves—feeling almost protective and nurturing at those versions. Reminiscing at the simplicity and ease of life—education, emotions, and relationships—our youth quietly seeps into our skin and we suddenly feel as vibrant and joyous as before. Feeling safe in the company of those who knew us at our gawky, nerdy, and asocial ages, we dance with abandon, pull each other's legs, and allude wickedly to embarrassing secrets and gaffes. Drifting into smaller groups, we don't realise we have naturally, and without thought, meandered to the clusters of "besties" of college days.

Alas, as with all other good things, the reunion also peters down to an end, and people start dwindling. A few passionate souls stay till the wee hours when the venue is closing down, promising most vehemently to meet soon and stay in touch. Will it happen? Guess not till many years pass by, and another wave of nostalgia sweeps in.

8

Marriage or the Lack of It

FROM friendships, the inevitable corollary is relationships and marriage. Possibly prompted by the reunion and rekindled friendships.

At times as a consequence of midlife crisis, or possibly a cause of crisis or through a deliberate decision post unpleasant experience, singledom pervades. It could be a deliberate choice or a collateral damage. As a singularly eye-opening passage, we witness how the middle-aged juggle this late dismantling of their marital status with single parenting and their own need for romance. Or how the middle-aged single rally valiantly and astutely the back and forth of questioning of their singledom.

And then there are those who have lasted, endured, and made it through, married as before—happily. Indeed, an applaudable achievement.

Crossing over in middle-ages

So, here is a new consequence that many in the previous generation did not have to face—the *deliberate* single. What I mean by deliberate is remaining unmarried or getting divorced by choice.

Shhh, lets slink to the quiet corner, come on you can tell me….haven't you thought once or more about running away and the closer you are to completing or crossing a decade of marriage, the more active that little voice must have been!

On a serious note, what makes some cross that marriage line never to return? What makes others contemplate crossing the line but never doing it, and still others to cross the line but return to the marriage? Well, maybe "crossing over" has less to do with the marriage and more to do with self-esteem and independence of thought. The other thing that decides whether the crossing over will actually happen, be permanent, or only temporary, depends on a person's definition of thresholds.

Having known a few at close quarters who stayed despite jolts to the "non-negotiables", their possible reasons have been a result of much introspection and soul searching. Some rationale after the soul searching:

- Maybe thresholds had not yet been breached. They were convinced that these were sporadic incidents and would not be repeated. Maybe they consider it one lost moment in the many happy memories.
- Or maybe there was a stronger underlying motivation behind returning and staying in the cocoon. Just that—marriage is a cocoon. Why is it so? Well, several reasons…

  a. It secures
  b. It stabilises

c. It supports
d. It gives you confidence to enter a roomful of people on the arm of your other half!
e. Or simply, there is another witness to this life that you have led.

- Last and probably the most important, financial interdependence—rules of the financial kingdom seem to be encouraging partnerships rather than singlehood in more than one way. It's just a lot easier to keep joint assets than waste the rest of your life trying to tear them apart.
- And for some, the spouse is a habit—you get used to having the person around and frankly, living without them seems more bothersome than with them. Or they show signs of mellowing down, mending, and the comfort of them staying as a habit is too important to break.

I do not mention children as a reason to cross over or stay since it is a short-lived reason—the way they grow, it is not long before they are building their own lives.

There aren't any right or wrong ways. What works for you need not work for others and vice versa. However, it is important to recognise the reasons for crossing over or staying and realise that it is not just a mere rationalisation, but something you truly believe in from the heart.

So, all I have to offer is that it is best to be honest with yourself, accept the decision taken, and shut the inner voice forever! Happy separation or happy married life—whatever state you chose, make your peace, fellow sis/bro.

The deliberate single ones

Again, unlike generations past, there are many of us who chose to stay single even as they enter or are in the throes of middle-ages. Why? Well, each has their legitimate reason. And even if we are lonely, solitude seems to be a better choice than an unhappy partnership.

Maybe they are once bitten and twice shy, maybe they like the freedom of their singledom or maybe they are still waiting. Having crossed the late 20s and 30s where the compulsion to be hitched seems to be the most, 40s and 50s relax this need into a wait and watch mode.

Or maybe the tiring task of finding mature love just seems daunting....why do I say that? Read on.

Seeking mature love

Sandwiched (there's the word again) between singledom and empty nests or maybe between singledom and onsetting years, you wonder what it would be like to date again, to try and find a companion again. Speaking from a woman's point of view (I am sure it holds true for men too), between weight issues, menopause, and reading glasses, it is a bit challenging to catch the eye.

Before I get labelled as a body shamer, anti-feminist, ageist, etc., I ask for your forgiveness in advance and am merely reflecting the thoughts that float around when you embark on yet another journey of the middle-ages. Having undergone, for many, debilitating divorces and separations, you may find yourself bewildered, jostled at cross-roads again—"how the **** did this happen to me?"

"Mature" love is, I guess, a politer way of saying that you have stepped off the "right" age to finding love and are now re-entering the journey, lessons learnt and readied to the older life stage. Diligently and delicately, you whisper hints to your friends, nudging them to see who is available in their circle, also hoping they can talk to the eligible on your behalf. You wait, you continue the nudges till they equally delicately revert with—"don't know anyone" or "don't know if you would find him/her suitable." In short, they swim away like slimy fishes, or so it feels.

Cafes, bars, and parties—you contemplate and maybe even try them as searching grounds. When all fails, you go online—dating apps, online events, and platforms, etc. Having heard many success stories, you fail to recognise that those successes are probably 1% of the innumerable failed attempts. In case you do happen to come across interesting and authentic profiles, the heart plunges when you notice the desired age group—"50-year-old seeking 25-35 age group". Seriously?! Leave them alone to get their own age groups. A few wise middle-aged men and women warn in advance—"we are not open to being sugar daddies or sugar mommies(?)" Yet, it is amazing the number of youngsters reaching out and spamming your profile while your own peer group remains tantalisingly out of reach.

It is challenging to take that hairpin bend to the road to partnership as you deal with your own insecurities, handle people "liking" and then "unmatching" you with grace, and then, with less grace, accept that a few are not going to want a second date with you. You may question why older men with "lines of experience" partner with women half their age, and the woman feels more inhibited doing so. You question if wisdom, companionship, and peace is less important than glamour, youthfulness, and excitement. Come on, isn't the answer obvious—of course the latter, duh! Ok, ok, let's not generalise or get cynical here—exceptions are always around.

Undaunted, you start yet again, discarding sources and apps that haven't worked and trying other modes—maybe an elite matchmaking service? Now that's a thought. Knowing the number of single and divorced people out there, I may start one of my own. Anyone interested?

Middle-aged marriage

Here is the other face of mature love—the surviving middle-aged marriage.

I recently come across the term "companionate love" which typifies intimate and committed marriage of the middle-ages, but not really passionate.

Hmmm, also running this past a few friends in this zone. Pause… a few days later… Yes, it is confirmed—this is true. They agree…

So, how would one describe marriage of the fortunate few who have stayed married after twenty-odd years and predict another twenty, at least for the foreseeable future? Realistically speaking, it could be called a peaceful co-existence, and optimistically speaking, it could be called an empowering partnership. In both cases, the common denominators seem to be giving each other space, respecting the spouse's priorities, interests, and most importantly, finally accepting over the years that this is how he/she is built.

The underlying theme seems to be of commitment, assuming no non-negotiables are crossed. Like one of my male friends, aged fifty, said, "It is just too much of an effort to have an extra-marital affair." He admitted that he has been tempted, but had too much respect (or maybe fear?) for his spouse and marriage to cross this non-negotiable. Instead, he chose to understand why he was getting tempted and indulged in other, less harmful feel-good activities, like canvassing geographical boundaries around the globe.

Another predictor seems to be how easily you accept that your spouse will want to experiment, spend money on meaningless past times that may just be indulgent and unproductive, and prefer male/female bonding with friends over spending time with you. Well, at least some of the time. Trust in your spouse; a little bit of lethargy and a very realistic assessment of both your charms, all help in acceptance.

Again not to body shame or be judgmental, but really, the wrinkles, slightly burgeoning tummy, and losing patches of hair as you face the mirror fill you with gratitude for your better half, who is probably in the same shape. This becomes even more critical when you think of the grown or growing children, no longer a reason for a sustained marriage. Not that children need to be a reason for being in a miserable marriage, but you will agree, they do make the years pass by swiftly.

It is also not only about a habit or familiarity or even the comfort of knowing another so well, but a little more intimate than that. There is opportunity for romance, intermittent passion, and closeness, the only difference being there is no urgency, status update, or mandated expectations now. Things become free flowing, less stressed, and just simply as per convenience. Sounds unexciting? Not really, just that the excitement tempers to intimacy. Sounds comforting and peaceful? Yes, any day.

At the end, it is how easily you and your spouse complement each other, seamlessly fill the crevices of each other's weaknesses and decide, very deliberately, that it is still worthwhile being together than apart.

You have juggled single parenthood

As a corollary to the deliberate choice of being single, let me also elucidate the travails of a single parent—my state and what I observed. A bit of a flashback here....

As we all sat around in the comfortable drawing room of a friend discussing parenting, domestic help, real estate prices, and work–personal life balance—the staple diet of all get-togethers and social conversations, I contributed intermittently and mostly observed.

With a sigh of resignation, I realised that I had drifted off again choosing to ignore the hackneyed discussions around. The others were discussing in the same opinionated voices, same arguments between the spouses, same stances: "You don't come home on time and don't know the hard work I put into looking after the kids"; "I get home from a stressful day, you at least have domestic help, so why are you complaining?", etc.

Suddenly, I was jolted out of my reverie, someone had asked me a question. I rarely offer an opinion as it is usually very different from what others are comfortable with, but since I was actually asked, I had no choice. "You must not be facing any such arguments as you are single, no?" To my mind, that was one of the most insensitive statements I have ever heard. Thankfully, one sensible friend laughed and pointed out, "She's probably gone through worst, which is why she is single, so let's not ask her about facing mere arguments!"

My children and I have gone through many years of growing up together. I have even had conversations with my fourteen-year-old on how the business needs to be handled. And I have had a discussion with my ten-year-old about why a family of three is as normal as the conventional four-member family, or how the children need to make decisions at a very early age. Sometimes I gave them early exposure to spiritual learnings too (what is tarot, how does hypnotherapy help, what is numerology, etc.), because they have seen you turn to these sciences for help and healing.

Of course, there were enough "normal" conversations and sibling fights too.

And then, of course, are the teachers who very diffidently ask will the "other" parent be coming for the PTM (parents–teachers meet)? They are clearly unsure and uncomfortable with the single mom phenomena and waver between sympathy and discomfort. So, my immediate response would be to tell them I am happily separated and that the children are quite comfortable with me being their sole representative.

Of course, I was later lynched by the children, their teachers wanted to know their history and started to treat them a little differently.

Added to this is the single working-parent issue. There is minimum fuss about food eaten, no time for pickups and drops from extracurricular classes. Teachers and hobbies are selected on the basis of convenience and price. Home delivery and home tuitions are a boon!

Given the above, I chose a parenting style which was flexible, low on pressure, and high on friendship and frankness. I chose to talk to them as adults, talk to them about most activities, decisions, and influences in my life so that there was always honesty between us. I chose a style wherein the kids were making big decisions independently, with minimum guidance.

Maybe as result, children of single parents are a little needier for genuine affection, a little quieter since introspection has started at an early age. But I do believe the early lessons of life that they learn make them more tolerant, relaxed human beings who value relationships and a larger family much more. Hopefully, they learn that affection and caring can come from many sources, and it is okay to be different.

The point of this entire flashback is that as a single parent, one starts becoming very flexible and accommodating of changing circumstances and needs. There is no one to ask and seek advice from and demands are plenty, so conventional wisdom just does not work in parenting!

9

The Next Big Crisis

THE mid-life crisis pales in comparison to this one—when the children grow and fly away. Leaving behind a huge, yawning gap that just cannot be filled. What the middle-aged parents go through, how they cope with this crisis and create new rules of parenting shows the inner strength that is the hallmark of middle-ages. Of course, having a great sense of humour, a thick skin, and fellow compatriots helps.

Empty nest

I question—when those we love deeply, viscerally, move on and make their own lives, is it time to let them go or go with them? Are you then an impediment or a support? Are you the stable base they look for as they flounder? Or are they the home you seek?

Teetering on the edge of childhood, on the brink of adulthood, one faces the looming empty nest with a feeling of your heart being ripped out from the body. How does one ever accept this emptiness or fill this yawning gap? Or should we look at it as a beautiful transit to spend some time in our own company?

As these empty nesters reach out to the larger community, it hits home that others are terribly busy creating their own temporary abodes, and this pastime can take a lifetime. Maybe they are happily settled into this routine and do not have to face gaps or vacuums. Maybe they do not allow voids into their lives. Maybe their roots go so deep, like trees staying upright, that transitionary influences do not affect them as deeply.

Meanwhile, as an empty nester, I take comfort from my table, my chair, my laptop, and my books. Are these then the only anchors? Words? Yes, this does anchor me to some extent—this need to keep writing feels as important as breathing. I am nothing without my words. A little sunshine, pots of flowers, a fully functional, completely charged laptop—all of this feels like a shore.

For others like me, their hearth, their hobbies, their work, or interests may become stable shores, and for a while, this is enough.

Here are some lasting words for those still grappling with the yawning gap of empty nests…

"I wouldn't coax the plant if I were you.
Such watchful nursing may do it harm.
Let the soil rest from so much digging
And wait until it's dry before you water it.
The leaf's inclined to find its own direction;
Give it a chance to seek the sunlight for itself.
Much growth is stunted by too careful prodding,
Too eager tenderness.
The things we love we have to learn to leave alone."

~ Naomi Long Madgett

The "new" parent

Paradoxically, all the rationalisation and the philosophical stances eulogised in the last piece just vanish into thin air, and the umbilical cord tugs hard. Your maternal feelings overwhelm you like the surge of a high tide wave. So, without much further ado, you respond to the call. Packing your bags, you buy the tickets within or outside the country and set off. Imagining the pleasant surprise and happy tidings ahead, you somehow tolerate the long journey to international lands, if that is where the children are.

Somewhere within the deep recesses of your brain, there is a niggling voice which whispers, "*are you sure your son/daughter wants you around? Is it fine? Was his/her voice just a little hesitant?*" But you hastily brush the voice aside, "*Don't be ridiculous, of course they are happy to receive you.*" Watching the movie, "Otherhood" on the flight does nothing to reduce the misgivings.

Humming a happy tune, you set off in the cab from the airport. It is a working day, but the tickets were cheaper, so obviously your child can't pick you up. Arriving with suitcases full of home goodies, foods, and other delights, you reach your child's apartment and wait patiently for him/her to arrive. Turning a blind eye to the mess inside the apartment, you resist the urge to clean up, mindful of the fact that this is his/her home, not yours.

As you tour around, you see some very apparent indicators of other occupants in the residence—clothes, personal care products, etc., of the opposite gender. Or you notice some products that are unexpected, not hidden very well, you know e-cigarettes, alcohol, etc., which theoretically you had knowledge of but still makes you cringe in reality. "Never mind, he/she is an adult now and know what they are doing. Anyway, don't interfere or say anything, okay?" you tell yourself. Reluctant to call and disturb your child at work, yet responding to the strident maternal call, you search the kitchen and decide a home-cooked meal is needed.

The bell rings and you rush with open arms to greet your child. Happy to see you yet slightly embarrassed, more so if it's your son, your child hugs you and the next few hours go off chattering about what is happening back home and your cascading questions about his/her life. "Ta da!" with a wave of flourish you reveal the painstakingly-made meal. Your son/daughter gives a weak smile as he/she reveals, "Mom, I usually eat at the office." "Oh, I didn't know.... never mind, I will eat it over the next few days or if you want, we can invite your friends over," you chirp, dismissing your disappointment.

Few days in and you and your adult child reach an understanding about what he/she likes, how he/she keeps their home, what are their hours, etc. After a few skirmishes and arguments about the differences in your way and their way of using the washing machine, quantity of detergent, stacking the dishes in the dishwasher, cleaning the apartment, and so on and so forth, new rules are laid down.

Visibly swallowing your critical advice, you realise a few home truths...

- The cuckoo has really flown the nest.
- Right or wrong, they have their own way of maintaining their sanctity.
- They were not a guest in your home, but you are.

- They lived by your rules and now you have to live with theirs, at least while in their apartment.
- They walked unannounced into your bedroom; you cannot do the same.
- No matter how cool and young at heart you are, and their friends may agree, after a while they want their space—alone. So better to take off for a long walk, a movie, visit relatives, etc.
- If you are here for a long stay, you know, like 2–3 months, give periodic breaks of privacy.
- Quickly find your way around, using the Uber rides, maps etc., to visit tourist spots or any other entertainment avenues as your working child is unlikely to find the time or energy beyond a point.

Last but not the least, do realise that while unconditional love is and will always be there, the urge to meet and be with your child was first and foremost your need, not so much theirs. Respond to it by all means and so will they, yet know that the neediness or clinging of a nostalgic relationship where their sun rose and set with you, has changed to be a more subtle, less urgent underlying relationship.

Time to cut the umbilical cord, dear, but rest assured, the strings of the heart will always stay connected.

We are all in it together

Just when you think you have the new parenting honed to a fine craft, time says "woah, not so fast". There is a new pandemic (apologies for the choice of the word given Covid times) in the family—self-discovery. Just when you feel you have the right, the space, and the mind to restage yourself, your grown-up/almost grown-up children, and your parents/in-laws, also want to do the same. After all, they are learning from you—both generations.

Oh no, here we go sandwiched again.

We make sense of our growth, changing hormones, and life stage, and somehow are also the encyclopaedias that help the other two generations make sense of theirs. So, the parents get into a complaining stage where the world around is an evil place, where worry is as important as breathing, and reassurance is a constant need. The youth are hassled, rebelling against any kind of authority, making sense of their college or working lives, and hence also in a complaining mode. Somehow both generations agree on one thing—blame your generation for all wrongs.

You, on the other hand, are completely forbidden from making any complaints or even asking for help in unravelling your own reformation. Go to a therapist, or, if you are lucky, find those sympathetic like-minded friends. Trips to the bathroom become your favourite jaunt and bath-time just gets longer. You read self-help books surreptitiously and seriously consider starting a support group—"the sandwich years".

Finding the middle ground (no pun intended), reassuring fears, subtly pushing youngsters to the right decision (while making them feel they decided), and sneakily googling for answers—these become your mainstays. Introspection is your solution. When? Run to the nearest jogging path, tennis court, swimming pool, or just long walks—use your exercise time wisely—body and mind muscles served.

Hope you reach the right paths.

Advise or not?

In continuation with the self-righteous rein of injustice in parenting, here is another one—if you thought there were terrible twos, I give you the confounding 20s. So here are the paradoxes, dilemmas….

- Suggest something and, "you are instructing", do not suggest then hear, "you are ignoring me."
- If you ask, "you are prying", if you do not ask, then, "you are disinterested."
- Greet and talk to their friends—"you are trying too hard", if not—"you are not cool."
- Constructive criticism is misconstrued as "gaslighting", praise is now "patronising."
- Ask favourite dishes or food to cook, and they feel "burdened", do not ask, well then either you eat everything and add to your burgeoning belly or discard.
- Wake them up and you are "mothering" them, do not wake them up, they are frantically blaming you for their delay
- Girlfriend/boyfriend issue discussions strictly on their initiative but any advice is too "biased and pessimistic."
- Work related advice is shelved as "outdated, too philosophical or impractical", yet they want the "wisdom of work experiences."

Hope you have got the gist of it. Parenting those between 20–25 years—range can get extended depending on familial relationships, growth of child etc.—is perplexing to say the least. In retrospect, the terrible twos seemed easier, at least you just needed to chase them physically, now you chase them figuratively, emotionally, and end up, well, gaslit yourself.

Between grandparents and grandkids

Given the effort and strategy we put in, it's really not fair how easily grandparents and grandchildren form and sustain a bond while we struggle to maintain the relationship threads. Slight exaggeration there, but as you look at your parents indulging, forgiving, and pandering to the whims of the grandkids, you shake your head and wonder… "Where was this person when I broke that expensive vase, when I failed the Math test, or went to a late-night party with boys? And kids, where was the love when I asked for a little help in the kitchen, the hot water bag, or a nice cup of tea?"

Money flows easily and smoothly from grandparents to grandkids. Gifts are given without any real reason, shorter, fancier party clothes are bought without protest, junk food is welcomed as often as asked, and "friends" of the opposite gender are conversed with easily. Video games are encouraged and may even be learnt. Granny stays awake, uncomplaining, to open the door late at night; grandpa arranges luxurious hotel stays, gap years from work or college are understood, and there is no pressure to start working—"after all, these are their years to enjoy life." Huh?

A short flashback of our parents to us:

- "Top grades are a must; all entertainment will be curtailed till you get those."

- "I will pick you up at 10 p.m. from the party. Don't care if it started at 9 p.m."
- "Nail that interview. How much does it pay? Get that job."
- "Isn't that dress a little short, a little revealing, a little too tight?"
- "Eat your veggies, and avoid potatoes like the plague."
- "You cannot miss college/work even for a day. What if there are consequences?"
- "Read books. Don't waste time on video games."
- "You will get that music CD, speakers, etc., when you achieve something."

Present times—children to us:

- "I am on the phone."
- "Mom, don't talk like that, they are old." (did you get the irony?)
- "Mom, you really need to move on."
- "I am tired (after all the partying and roaming around). Can't you do this for me?"
- "I have worked over ten hours today. I am exhausted." (Just saying, we are still working)
- "Why do I need to do anything? I am on vacation."
- "College is really hard now; we need to compete a lot more than you guys did."
- "I need to look trendy. Image is important, unlike in your times."

Need I go on? So, I have two hypotheses to explain this bonding of the two generations while we are squeezed in the middle. One, your parents are becoming aware of the mistakes they made while parenting you and guilt-indulge your children. Two, they feel less responsible. After all, you are there to pick up the pieces from the aftermath, so they feel free to enjoy the relationship.

In terms of your children, both the hypotheses hold. Children are somewhere aware that they are short-changing you, but cannot let go of the reins of control lest you over-expect. Second, grandparents are your responsibility too, so kids feel free to enjoy their company.

Irrespective of the hypothesis, I must say, I do feel a little resentful—wait till I become a grandparent! Revenge will indeed be sweet.

10

The New Us

AFTER all the jostling, life turns to be a cycle, and what a ride it has been. The middle-aged has, at last, metamorphosed. We finally understand that life has to be revisited, some dramatic changes have happened and now it's time to leverage the gains. In short, start afresh, look ahead, and learn to juggle the past with the future.

The next 1300 odd weeks of life…

Yet, ironically, it takes the youth to give you some new perspectives.

A casual conversation with the younger kith and kin revealed a startling insight—life suddenly feels shorter if counted in weeks. All your unfulfilled dreams and wishes rush to the fore clamouring for attention. The insight—an innocent statement enumerating the number of weeks one has left in life, no matter how big the number, it still creates a precariously imposed momentum. Suddenly there is mayhem inside and you rapidly churn out your plans and goals for quick redemption.

Another big realisation that dawns is that you are your best company at this time or as good as shifting emotions allow you to be. To keep things on an even keel, humour really is not only the best but the only medicine.

When the number of 1300 weeks was shared with peers, understandably there were fervent discussions on the need for a new avatar. And, emerged the following list of things to adhere to now....make your own list fellow mid-lifers.

1. Avoid the newspaper—or read the front page (and the cartoons) just to keep up the semblance of being informed.
2. Travel even more—use those beautiful discounts, packages, offers, etc. Currently, these lip-smacking offers seem cruel, like trapping a child and then luring him/her out with delicious candy.
3. Take a break from Zoom. We are becoming so efficient, carbon footprints and all, but if I need to see that insipid screen with people reduced to pictorial boxes or, at the best, jumping diffused faces anymore, I will scream. Saturation has been reached and then some...
4. Do not discuss ill health in all its gory details and messes—so many closet hypochondriacs are now in the open and the declared ones should really put a lid on it, lest they lose all control over their brain.
5. Do not use any references to 2020 as the doom year, unusual year, the year of reckoning or any such high-handed, all-knowing description. We honestly have no bloody clue why the hell this happened and what

the lessons are. All one knows is that one day we were travelling or dreaming of holidays and malls and enjoying the rewards of steady jobs, and the next day it was all over in one lockdown month.

6. Try not to complain about the traffic jams, human noise, crowds, and over population—the day traffic started crawling back on roads and a few brave people precariously stepped out of the road, I did heave a huge sigh of relief. One of those lockdown evenings when I had stepped out on the road for a walk (I know, I know it was against the rules, but it was either that or jumping out of my skin), I swear, I thought an apocalypse had hit the town and I was the only human alive.
7. Invite friends over. No, let me rephrase, force friends to come to your home or call us over. It is my firm conviction that humans are not meant to be isolated. It feels as comfortable as self-immolation. Starved of human interaction outside families, we are now remarkably familiar with every expression, body language cue, and sound emitted by our loved ones.
8. WFH and WTF—the two seem interchangeable—pardon my French! For a person who deliberately chose to be a work-from-home employee, this now has the appeal of an imprisonment at Alcatraz. We need to choose it, not be forced into it. It was once an act of rebellion but now is the new normal.
9. And then another of the oft-repeated phrases—digitisation. I doubt if the great learning from life is that we all need to become robotic imprisoners of more

machinery, artificial intelligence, and that impersonal, void called "online" will ever replace the sheer pleasure of human interaction and feel of terra firma.

This list and rant, as you will notice, can become endless so one has to be limited by the 1300 odd weeks. Take out that bucket list and kickoff!

Fun

Have you been bogged down by the earnestness and seriousness of life? Decided to be a martyr and consider fun to be a world outside your territory of middle-age and motherly/fatherly/spousal duties? Then you sorely need it.

After all there is no need to burst a blood vessel lugging our soft bodies up the mountain of responsibilities or collapse from the lifeforce draining to-do lists of life. So, how about getting a bit of that second wind and re-considering what exactly constitutes fun for you? I did a small "survey" amongst middle-aged friends and here were some interesting activities; and safe to say, interests define fun…

Most of them interlinked relaxing and creative stimulations as fun. Music, dance, painting, cooking became an aspect of fun. Then there were the proactive, fast-paced activities like aerobic exercises, trekking, travelling, power walks. Yet, for others it was coffee with friends, going for movies with friends, reading books, golfing with friends (no, not the ones where it is more about clinching business deals and networking), hanging out with family, and binging on OTT platforms. A few lamented about how they no longer could finish books without dozing off (I do the same with TV programs) or having the time to pick up new skills. Learning new languages and meeting new friends were new aspects of fun.

And then there is the entire gamut related to alcohol and the repercussions thereafter. However, unlike the yesteryears, it is more about discovering the learning of alcohol and less about consuming it. So, fun is making fancy cocktails at home, finding new places to drink and new friends to drink with, discovering the antique drinks, or just deciding to drown in the knowledge of some drinks. The repercussions are of course varied, but some mentions of Blackjack, Poker, and myriad gambling indulgences do emerge.

Fun for me, is a more blissful time, you know the kind where you drift into nothingness, watching the sunset as you luxuriate in your gently swinging hammock.

In a nutshell, fun was really anything that did not require too many grey cells, or hard efforts yielding success, excellence, or huge amounts of money. Nor was it about work or sources of income—hah, funny that! Absolutely no one said their work is fun! We have been spending 8–12 hours if not more for the past three decades, thinking, doing things that are no fun. Blasphemy, I say!

Fun is created, not given

On the topic of fun, where are the stimulating outlets for men and women over 50? Barring the soporific coffee chats, there seems to be limited fun events for older men and women. One of the advantages of InterNations that I had joined at Chicago, and I suspect that is how it is globally, was the predominance of middle-aged people. And they were not boring.

However, in the community at large, pubs, dancing sessions, gaming parlours, bowling arcades, and such physically-active fun places seem to be the territory of youngsters. Join any of these barring pubs, and you can see the youth sniggering behind their hands. Hey! we may be older, but we are equally zestful.

On sheer stubbornness, I joined a Zumba class which claimed to be catering to all ages but had only those between 20–30 years. The pace, the tempo, and the complete lack of teaching left me paralysed and I never went back. Ok, so I admit, our pace and skills may be a little less, but we can still have fun.

In the end, we are left to our own devices—we create our fun times but unfortunately mostly they are dinners, get-togethers, and slow heritage walks. And for heaven's sake, discussing ambitions of grown-up children, real estate, stocks, and business is not fun! *Yawn*. How about those treks, bowling competitions, long road trips, sailing into the sunset, dancing to Bryan Adams, and other talents of our times—who is game?

We don't really have to wait for the 50th birthday celebrations or any special occasion to have stimulating fun—it can be a part of any day, every day.

To quote from the movie, "Before Sunset"—"when you satisfy one desire, you agitate another."

Travelling leaps ahead

One of the most pleasant side-effects of the middle-ages is travel—in fact it is one of the best lingering benefits of working life.

Travel is one of the few things that beats all lethargy and laziness out of the laxest middle-aged. This is actually the best decade to travel. You have more or less taken care of the most pressing of duties and parental deeds, that house has finally been built, and the instalments are going smoothly. Work can be delegated, and really the world will not collapse if you take off for a couple of weeks, unlike in previous decades.

So, you plan jauntily, book the best resorts; of course, you take flights everywhere, well, there are a few daring Harley-Davidsons also out there. You are excited about new places to see. Experiences, stories, visual treats, culture, history—all of these inspire, as do sometimes even the people.

Next comes preparing a list of all the stakeholders involved in this decision—you know, you *are* taking off for two weeks to travel to Europe or Antarctica or whichever intriguing corner of the world beckons. First comes the team, then the emails notifying your absence, the auto response for your inbox and answering machines.

If you are self-employed then woe begone, there is no one to delegate to, and clients/investors look at you with arched eyebrows. "Really? You want a vacation at this time?" Closing your eyes, the inspiring tug of travel still pulls, and straightening your spine, you spit out a terse "yes." Really, one would think going into a battle was easier.

At last, the day arrives and the child in you is jumping with excitement. If with family, you have the pleasure and the pain of sharing your travel moments with them. If not, well aren't you the lucky one… I can see you rubbing your hands in glee.

Armed with your language dictionary and *Lonely Planet* book, you set off and suddenly everything expands inside of you. Eager to learn, camera hoisted, a writing pad (writers like me), bottle of water, and maybe some snacks, you and your backpack are off. Oh, the prospect of getting lost, not communicating in a known language, making friends with cab drivers and guides, and the hotel or resort staff in your new home. If camping or hiking is your thing, then the mountains, forests, and rivers all gather to guide you. It seems like the whole universe inspires your travel.

Happy journeys, middle-aged!

Solo trips

On the heels of travelling comes Solo trips. It has taken you three decades to leave the self-conscious 20s behind and emerge this confident avatar who is happy to travel alone. In fact, may even prefer it.

More men and women this age want to travel solo for leisure. As a part of the "solo trip for women over 50s" Facebook (can't get myself to call it Meta) groups, I notice what an effort it seems to be for middle-aged women across the world to make that decision and implement it. They worry over their image if seen dining alone at a restaurant, their safety (which is legitimate), and their adult children worry even more.

Most seem to embark on solo trips as a celebration or a rebellion, depending on the mindset, post a betrayal, divorce, or some other tragic happening. Not to say that there are no happy solo travellers or those with husbands are content to lounge at home, watching TV. Maybe the ones who voice their triumph of solo trips are more of those recovering from trauma.

Needless to say, the more exotic and adventurous the destination, the more you want to do it alone. Somewhere in the middle-ages, with the passing of time, remote locations for solo trips seem to be the call of the wild.

I remember my trip to Rome (not so adventurous, I admit) that I selected for my first solo sojourn. It was lovely. I got lost, obviously as couldn't understand the signs and am pretty directionally-challenged with the map. So, I had to scour the areas on my own to reach the tourist spots. Pretty soon, I had strangers walking up to me asking for directions! Nothing like getting lost to discover a city.

The rewards I got were equally lovely. Standing in the queue to see "The Mouth of Truth" (*Bocca della Verità*) at the portico of the Santa Maria in Cosmedin church, I was presented with a rose by an elderly man in front of me. Everyone was carrying roses to place at the altar of Mother Mary. Saying the words *belladona* (beautiful lady), he gallantly presented me the rose even while his wife looked on indulgently. What a welcome to the city!

PART TWO

UNRAVELING THE RAMBLINGS

Making sense of this journey with Revelations, Questions, and Remedies ….

What Did We Accumulate Along the Way?

YOU can be very sure that along the journey to the middles, you would have accumulated a lot. I don't mean physical things, though I am sure your storage garage, storage room, racks, lofts, and cupboards at friends' homes would have a story to tell on those hoardings. That aside, what other things have you accumulated? I know that when I hit fifty, I realised there were a lot of memories, emotions, hurts (some presumed), and unrealised dreams that I was expounding to anyone that cared to listen.

What we accumulate along the way really projects how heavy or light our luggage is. It would be good if we could open our suitcase of memories, wants, and dreams and remove some of the unwanted, unnecessary stuff. Similar to the way we struggle with our wardrobes—you know, those heart-wrenching moments when we throw away the old jeans we have clung to in the vain hope that we can fit back into them.

You really can't enter the mid-ages with a heavy baggage. There will be many memories that your fogged brain will not remember, thankfully, but others, you will have to sort through and see what can be safely discarded, happily or otherwise. Just as those jeans will never fit you again, some dreams also need to be discarded pronto.

So, hereon are the revelations, learnings, questioning, suggestions, and actions that the journey to the middle-ages evokes. Read on for more insights and a set of actions to leap ahead with. To make them look contemporary and millennial, I have hashtagged them (still no idea how they work).

REVELATIONS

Some insights, some *ahaa* moments, and mostly important learnings we gathered…

#1

We are still works in progress

As I sat to count my achievements, there are two things I did, first—eliminated all sources of disturbances, and wiped my brain clean of worries.

Counting the pats on my back, I searched desperately in the crevices of my pasts and present, and realised that most of them are intangible and inward. Nevertheless, let me list down the learnings....

- I am trying to cultivate a sense of humour—can at times be dark, at times sarcastic, but mostly, wry and self-deprecating humour that makes me take myself less seriously.
- I am in the process of building a filter that can sieve what comes out of my mouth—mostly, hard opinions, criticism, stubborn bone-headedness, and noise (metaphorical too)—like those noise-cancelling headphones. Just remember that excessive noise from you will make others wear them too, so don't say what you don't want to hear. Self-control of your words,

despite the ego pushing, is a massive achievement. It is ongoing so long as we are alive.

- Realising that I need not react to provocation, shouting, and adverse reactions in a similar vein.
- I am learning that serving others without having myself peaceful and indulged first, is an unnecessary sacrifice.
- I am trying to achieve the art of not adding to the surrounding chaos by maintaining a silence. Sometimes at the cost of biting my lip, allowing things to be, till it is necessary to actively do or say something.
- As a middle-aged responsible adult, I have realised that life is a circle, full of cycles. Hence, chasing the end of your tail will not break these cycles or circles, it will just keep you comfortable in the thought that you are headed somewhere. Take disruptive actions even if the consequences are scary, but remember to jump with a parachute over your head or have a safety net lest you fall. Try also to not break anyone else's bones in the process. If your actions can potentially harm or hurt another, they need a careful review and candid conversation.
- Respecting boundaries, becoming more diplomatic, and cultivating habits that make me look and feel good are not signs of hypocrisy or becoming less authentic, but possibly the only ways to thrive. If these steps can lead to better, healthier relationships as you create space for self and others, then why not?
- Lastly, I also chose silence over criticism, even if it makes me a hypocrite, as I realise I have absolutely no authority to criticise. Also, I understand that each is battling their

own insecurities and if they are indeed living in a fool's paradise, their reality will catch up with them sooner or later.

All in all, we are all works-in-progress, but the operative word is "progress". As long as you are self-aware and focused on building a strong, silent core, you are a far better contributing and productive individual than you know. As the external falters, the internal world becomes richer, more trustworthy, and predictable. I am deeply appreciative and humbled by the creative works that enable this process—books, music, art, etc. that inspire and lift us from the ordinary to the extraordinary.

So, what is your checklist of progress extraordinaire? Care to share your works-in-progress?

#2

Silence is the new speech

HOW do you wake up every morning?

Mulling over this question, I realise this has been one of my biggest learnings over the years. I try to wake up, if not with a spring in the step, then at least a smile on the face. I greet my handful of plants, relish my cuppa coffee, and for those few moments, life is good.

Then comes in the newspaper, the bustling visitors, the spate of doorbells and that beautiful sense of peace is lost, gone forever in the vistas of the busy ahead. In that brief panorama, you live a thousand moments of serenity.

So, I asked myself, what are the ways in which I can retain these moments and not be answerable to the dictates of the day? How can I rescue this time—this most prolific, most aware passage of my every day? And the answer was simple. Capture this mood, this expansiveness in one corner of your mind, to be retrieved at a moment's notice. Sounds difficult? It is not, you just need to commit it to memory, like we do other more mundane things in our life.

Have you ever had trouble remembering mobile numbers of your family, children, or important contacts? Not really, yet you struggle to create this one saved space in the crevices of your mind.

It gets recreated in silence—a silence that only the soothing whirring of the fan is allowed to accompany—that deep silence of what must exist in the universe as it hums its way to creation.

If you can feel that largeness and somehow can capture a stillness within you, then, all the interventions of daily humdrum will drop away like pinpricks on an elephant's skin.

I liken my everyday moments of communing in peace to the *motionlessness* that exists deep below the noises in the universe.

And suddenly, everything falls into place. As you reach the source of that tranquillity of creation that comes after destruction (in our mundane lives I would call them interruptions), you realise that you are in-charge and not the routines, the tasks, and the schedules of the day. *You* call the shots, and *you* decide when you will permit yourself to drift away.

The only memo is that every day, *summon that silence.* Visualise it like a deep, velvety humming galaxy akin to the sound of our own heartbeat that seems so still in the night, yet enfolds the harshest of destruction within it. Rather than calling it destruction, I call it reconstruction. For only when we reconstruct ourselves daily, do we design a meaningful day and life.

#3

We are finally free!

OH, the freedom! Oh, the carefree existence! Oh, the absolute lack of worry! Yes! I am finally on my way to absolute freedom…

The biggest, absolutely completely biggest corollary of turning fifty and over is the complete or nearly complete annihilation of the need to be on top of your game. Don't remember names—no worries, blame it on the aftermath of menopause. Don't remember appointments—it's the brain dwindling down. Remember the date of the boring party of your peers' discussing politics, economy, real estate…*yawn* and for obvious reasons don't want to go, no problem, it's the blasted recurring ache in the lower back.

And the best part is that no one really cares either—well, let's just say you no longer shine with your wit and personality either.

As you come to your own, you realise the liberating feelings of just not caring enough. Of course, you care about your dear ones and important things, but really, the list has grown a lot shorter. For example, it doesn't matter that your neighbour has better trimmed hedges and a blossoming garden while yours struggles to survive as you forgot to water them once again. And that your car has not been cleaned for some time and passersby have written graffiti on the dusty panes, including an instruction to clean it. It also really doesn't matter that you wore the same clothes to the last party—in your defence, this is the only set that lets you breathe. The list goes on and more gets added to it each year of midlife.

Oh, the relief of leaving the sensitivity of the twenties when every criticism felt catastrophic, when validation was like a fundamental right, sleepless nights were spent over imagined insults, and competition was a habit. Days were rosy, full of promises, and life seemed like the beginning of an exciting journey or they would be dismal, sad, and worrying. Nothing was balanced; both social and work life were equally hectic

Not to mention the exciting but overwhelming existence of the thirties—marriage, young kids, schooling demands, buying a home, mortgages, and loans (which in all fairness carries on till your brain is no longer working), worrying about promotions and career progress, salary packages, etc. Whew a really, really exhausting phase. I was glad when the decade of the forties arrived. At least you know how to cope with these stresses better, even as they start gathering critical mass and speed. And then suddenly it hits you—you are fifty years old!

The whites and greys of hair fight for attention amidst the sagging paunch and ahem, *cough*, other parts of the body. Yet hope lives strong—this is just temporary, minor hiccups in the path to regrouping the energy, figure, and skin of the early twenties.

You see, there is always a gap of two decades between the mind and the body.

Fifty hits home that the young upstarts at work are, well, upstarting you. Your children are waxing eloquently, on ways to survive the corporate world, the fast pace of technological upgrades, and a part of you is just sitting there, scratching your head—huh? I know, I know, it's not so bad. As I said, there are a large fortunate set amongst us who have been regularly taking their vitamin shots, exercising furiously, eating healthy with Spirulina organic, networking and hobnobbing with the rich and famous, etc., completely abreast with this new manic world.

Then there are these fifty-five-year-olds riding electric scooters, biking like the wind, and taking their Harley-Davidson out for long, strenuous mountain climbs. And then there are others (present company included), huddling further into the warm comfort of the quilt, complaining wholeheartedly about the chill of the winter, using any excuse to binge watch television.

Woah, not so fast. Grab the handrails, and don't descend onto the slippery slope—there is still time, so peek out of the quilt and run, okay, do power walks out in the sun.

Many of us expect that by the late forties or fifties, suddenly life will become easier. It seems like a magical number when life would be figured out. We would have retired from our tiring endless rat race and have a successful business of our own or at least an entrepreneurial stint. A good many do manage this—kudos for this brilliant achievement. The rest of us wait…

The silver lining for the fifties, along with developing a very thick skin, is that we can summon the energy, optimism, ambition, and carefree laughter of our youth at will, especially if time has been kind to us. Memories of how good achievement feels are still alive and kicking, just lying dormant till brought forth. The only difference is that now you know the cake from the icing, so use these precious resources for what truly matters.

Dreams are rekindled and plans for business are implemented with gusto and urgency, sensing that the next two decades can still be rescued within the broad ambits of health and strength. Some dreams are about work, some about hobbies; and some about creative endeavours making a late bloom. Irrespective of time seeming limited. We look forward eagerly for achievements of this new paradigm.

#4
We have mastered patience

"Nature does not run, it is not in a hurry, there is no haste... learn to be patient. If you can wait infinitely, it may even happen instantly. But you should not ask that it should happen instantly: if you ask, it may never happen. Your very asking will become a hindrance, your very desire will create a distance between you and nature. Even if takes ages to come, then too it is not late—it is never late. It always comes in the right moment."

—Osho, *When the shoe fits*

ALL the running, chasing, and racing comes to a screeching halt when you read these words. Try this—every morning with your cup of freshly brewed coffee/tea, walk out into the balcony and wish your handful of plants a happy morning. For those few seconds when you touch them and imagine they touch you too, there is peace in the heart. They ask for nothing and you need to give nothing—just an exchange of smiles.

Like with everything else in our lives, we fill our balconies or our small patches of gardens with every plant and flower that we can possibly get hold of. Deliberately limit to a few plants—each is then given the space and opportunity to grow and spread. For them to not get intertwined in each other's weeds or leaves, but to just grow in any direction they want.

It also enables you to take care of them and nourish \and treat every one of them individually, warranting of time and attention.

Patience is nothing but creating this space, this vacuum in between our rushed desires and tasks—a gap for nature to walk in and do its magic. Patience is allowing us the space and the calm to grow, to spread and to deliberate and then decide action.

There is a reason nature walks slowly and spreads slowly yet is not bored or distracted. *It is in deep surrender*. It experiences, feels, understands, and introspects every step as it moves. Nature is not stagnant, quite the opposite, actually. It feels movement everywhere, like changing weather from storms, droughts, blinding sun, and draining heat to healing showers, and crippling, dry winters. The core that keeps it going in the midst of ebbs and flows is patience.

If there is one thing that the middle-ages teach, it is patience. After decades of pushing and pulling, highs and lows, and weathering various storms and springs too, you realise that now, you can surrender. You can look back and see that there was always help at hand.

In this soothing space of patience, you also realise that the next fork in life, the remaining years, will teach you how to age gracefully. The tree of life will become sturdier, yet more frail, as the trunk will darken with the circumstances it has survived. Yet, it would strengthen even more till it becomes a rock.

From the growing, bright green and supple tree, you become a strong, loving rock—a hard, broad trunk that the younger trees, flying leaves, and grass below cling to for support.

Patience teaches you to become this old tree and not an ever-sprouting weed that rushes to capture every resource, every space, till it gets pulled out.

How do I picture patience? Sitting under that old oak tree, smiling at the surrounding plants in varying shades of green, conversing with them like friends in deep communion.

How do you picture patience? If you were to draw a painting called patience, how would you do so?

#5

We watch the boundaries

THOSE were the days when we could pretty much say what we wanted to say and get away with it. This statement would probably be true of the generation before ours—our parents and grandparents. Or maybe not. Confused? So am I.

I think every generation has learnt how to communicate to the younger generation the hard way. Amidst much agony, misunderstandings, and arguments, some patriarchal families still get away with possibly having zero filtering process, i.e., what they think is what they say.

What contributes to this caution is respecting boundaries. A big one, at that. Imitating our aging parents or even those 10–15 years older than us and then implementing their behaviour, comments, and instructions on our not-so-young children, you realise, is not working. The newer generations are big on boundaries—maybe not in social media, but definitely in terms of their individuality and independence. Maybe your parents still call and instruct you and feel it is their birthright to pry into your daily activities, but you cannot try that on your children.

Rightly so, I must say. The more we create boundaries and communicate them to others, the more we create space and respect for ourselves. Boundaries are not, however, shutting down or isolating yourself. But they definitely are ensuring that close ones know your likes and dislikes, what you will allow or disallow, and how much you want them to adhere to these boundaries.

For example, morning cup of coffee and ruminating, and being alone with my thoughts are an important time for me, and this has been communicated as such to near and dear ones. However, not everyone gets that, so they may still bombard you with calls and questions that are far removed from that ether world you have drifted into. What do you do? Well, you can ignore the calls, drift, or detach yourself mentally from the conversations and so on.

Many will not understand, let alone respect, your boundaries, as our close-bound Indian joint families are not culturally used to this. Nevertheless, these boundaries are important. Do not tolerate what feels like a violation in any way. Strong words, but sometimes it is important to let family members know this. We all know from personal experience that the younger generation is very quick and sharp in letting us know their personal boundaries, and that's definitely a page we can borrow from their books.

Here is a test for you—define your boundaries. Anything less than 5 will be penalised! And then the tough task—communicate them to all and sundry, ensuring they are adhered to for at least a month. Should we get started?

#6

Our young adults still need us

THERE is a happy realisation amidst the growing feeling of redundancy that the younger generation does indeed need us, though a changed version of us.

Transformation is the only solution. Not slight, minor adjustments, but a complete metamorphosis. Our youth want us to not preach, not give advice that dates 30 years back, but to walk with them. *Learn with them, yet observe and anticipate faster than them and then give advice.* They want us to continue to inspire them, lead them and guide them, but by adapting to current times.

Daunting task! As a sandwiched generation, we have a lot on our plates. But, if we do not evolve and learn to talk to our growing children in their language, live in their environment, and participate in their new lives—we will not be able to be in their lives. That is the stark truth. Not to say that they will not respect us or be emotionally there for us, but we may lose relevance faster than when it is inevitable.

Based on conversations with the younger generation that I have had, and with students I have taught and observed, here are my two bits on what I perceive as their requirements from us:

- First and foremost, be happy. If not happy, be calm. The younger generation feels flummoxed, guilt-ridden, and unhappy when they see their older family members, parents, etc., showing distressed emotional states. Not because they think we are unflappable or infallible, but because they feel helpless to save us.
- Treat them as equals and definitely worthy of interest, respect; and even as advisors to us. Believe me, their objectivity and fresh, new ways of looking at the world can be an eye opener.
- Allow them their lapses into childhood, tantrums, and other indicators of a young person trying to become an adult without judging, coddling, or advising them. They are as much entitled to these episodes as we middle-aged are allowed the wallows of self-pity occasionally.
- Do not assume they do not want us, need us, or are not emotionally calling out for help. Even if they do not ask for it; everyone needs support. Just be sensitive to that slight nuance, that midnight half-sleepy admittance to them missing us because that's all the hint you will get.
- Their working life, college life, and admittance into adult life is a huge step—walk with them as they step gingerly onto that bridge. Not ahead of them, but beside and maybe even behind, bolstering them.
- Feel inspired yourself to inspire them. They are constantly reviewing your actions, words, and observing you. Eerie,

no? Yet when they see you passionate, enthused, and inspired, they feel the same. When they see you being decisive, action-oriented, and hopefully jumping onto the bandwagon, they do the same.

- Learn from them about technology and social media use. Like making reels, podcasts, YouTube videos—okay, I admit the list is endless. Just make a start.
- Last and the most difficult, yes, they will make mistakes, and wrong choices. They are going to irritate you with their fluctuating moods and decisions, and drive you insane with their stubbornness over obvious lapses in judgments, but let them be. It will be painful to watch from the sidelines but still do allow it to happen. Provide the cushion, the parachute, and the strength when it happens because sometimes winning the argument is less important than nurturing the relationship.

#7

Shades of grey

THERE, that heading caught your attention, didn't it? Well, that was the intent. But before you let your imagination run away with you, this piece is not what you think! What I mean by shades of grey is a space between the black and the white. Sorry to disappoint…

Seriously though, I think the best coping mechanism is to know, that you really don't know. That you don't have a decisive or even correct answer to everything. Maybe not everything and everyone is what they appear to be. So that colleague/friend/family member who is always ready to take credit for your work or has disdained you in public, may admit to you in an inebriated moment that he/she is intimidated by you. Or that your know-it-all attitude irritates them or any other such lame reason, and suddenly everything is clear. I am not saying that the person will suddenly become your favourite person, but at least you will bring them into hues of grey.

Rarely do situations ask for very black and white judgments. Yes, murders, criminal acts, violence, emotional harm and similar acts do need them but otherwise, many situations or behaviours may fall into the zone of grey. Oh, the relief of not having to defend your black and white opinions, of the laziness of being a fence-sitter, of silently agreeing to disagree, the generosity of considering another's viewpoint.

Staying in shades of grey is not the same as being cowardly or a peacemaker or a people pleaser; but just agreeing that being open to different perspectives makes you more aware and adds to your growth.

Neither is being grey the same as being passive aggressive or sulking. Ambivalence is not a bad state, it is that transitional state where you are introspecting, observing, understanding, and possibly reaching a decision where all responses/opinions seem equally correct. After all, thankfully, we are not all lawyers and judges or serving in a jury, so why behave like one in day-to-day life? Even those in judiciary must be happy to not play that role outside of work.

If you have very strong and well-defined answers, it may silence people around you and mistakenly make you believe that they agree with you. But, maybe it could just be greys getting subsumed by the black—in other words, silence getting conquered by argumentative noises.

It is indeed good to know that the black and white barriers are falling and giving way to the softer greys and more compassionate beings. In the true spirit of being grey, I do feel that maybe this will not make the world unpredictable, but a world that respects free will as long as it does not hurt or harm another.

QUESTIONING

Now this is the deep end, the wretched overthinking brain wants to connect with the soul; so, it puts forth some very uncomfortable questions.

#1

Is self-preservation overrated?

MIDLIFE is an intersection in another way. Has life taught you self-preservation to the point of minimal risk? Or has it led you to become a person open to risks and action with a minimum sense of self-preservation? By no means am I disparaging the need for self-preservation, but I do think the thresholds differ from person to person. And each one has the right, actually the duty, to measure and adhere to their personal threshold.

What may seem like throwing caution to the wind or making a stubborn, headstrong set of decisions, could be routine for a more experimentative mindset. Maybe some of us are open to the possibility that the life purpose of most human beings is to act and assess the reactions or aftermaths. Life then is just a series of choices and experiments, all of which have a high likelihood of going wrong. But what if they went right, what then?

Midlife is a time where we realise that every decision, each choice made independently, was an experiment. Some worked and some did not. For those that worked, we were called successful, got approved and validated, and we attracted a courtier of admirers too. For those that did not work, we attracted naysayers, self-righteous pointing fingers, and nodding heads with the spoken or unspoken, "I told you so."

So, we went wrong? So what about it? What is the worst that could happen? We lose money, well, we get opportunities to earn it back. We lose dignity, well, we get opportunities to earn that back too, assuming that your sense of dignity lies outside of judgments.

I remember a time when I was interning as a recruiter for a leading BPO, and I interviewed a forty-year-old man who had experimented with a business and failed. To support his young family, he was seeking a job as a tele-caller. He showed no embarrassment for the failed business and was enthusiastic throughout the interview to do a job of a mere caller to irate clients. My admiration knew no bounds—his failures had not dented his passion for life, yet his self-preservation instinct was making him take a meagre job to support his family. If I recall correctly, that highly educated and experienced man did get the job and was overjoyed. I suspect not only due to the relief of finding a job but also responding to his need to experiment yet again.

Midlife is a time where you look back not to fear and build more self-preserving walls around yourself—perfect life with chauffeur-driven cars, villas in the best location, trophy designations and jobs—but to reduce the need for self-preservation and ask your heart: "Are there any more experiments left for me or this is it?"

Instead of becoming comfortable with the plush routine, is there some tiny corner in our lives where we can push the envelope a little? Where can we let go of the fortress of self-preservation and experiment without fear? If it makes you anxious, sets your heart beating at an unprecedented rate, and makes you seek the core strength inside of you without harming others, then go for it. True freedom lies in letting go, surrendering the controls of that experiment to the unknown, and seeing where it takes you.

Some can jump off the proverbial cliff without a harness or a parachute, while others need at least a tethered rope around their ankles. That is your personal threshold of surrender, but do try to jump off occasionally. Like I said, you could get badly hurt against the jutting rocks of the cliff, or you could have the most exhilarating flight of your life. Which one will it be?

Don't you think that after meeting all the obligations, creating the self-preserving security for your family and yourself, midlife can be a time when you can chase the unknown of that small experiment and see where it lands?

Let go and fly a little.

#2

Are you immersed?

WHAT have you immersed yourself in the most? What have you invested the most in? I do not mean money alone, I mean resources that include time, effort, emotions, energy, etc. Have these been scattered across various aspects of life such as work, family, and children—which is the usual case for most of us—or have a few directions been more immersive?

How much of your time and how many of your resources have you invested in solitude, immersing yourself in its calming shores? Have you thought of immersing yourself into nothingness? And while I know this is a much-espoused spiritual cliché, have you ever immersed in self-love?

"It is a lesson in immersing yourself in every aspect of interest. Know everything there is to know about it"

—Rod Judkins, *The Art of Creative Thinking*

What are the interests that you have sustained since your younger years or maybe revisited in your middle-ages? Immersion is really absorbing, being depthless. The more you know, the less you feel you know. Nothing about it makes it feel complete, and the curiosity to learn more, do more, in that interest grows incessantly. This then becomes a purpose, a self-satisfying goal that needs no external stimulation or validation.

Take your time, pick a few personal goals and then maybe tunnel it down to one or two. More than that would not really be immersion. The best part of this self-directed immersion is that it is very liberating. There is no need to prove you are an expert at it, there is no need for anyone else to know about it, and it is a journey that you take only with yourself. It could be creative, it could be intellectual, it could be physical, or maybe a combination of all three. The only demand it has is total immersion—an unabating devotion to it such that it withstands the tests of time, outside world, family, work, and so on.

Yet it is this very fiery focus that ironically creates the expertise you never sought. All of us are born creative and curious. The easiest way to bring back that inquisitiveness is to recollect your childhood days and maybe even ask your parents, siblings, or other people who have been with you since childhood, about what made you different from other children.

What were the interests, skills, and activities that engrossed you so much that you immersed yourself in them at the expense of the outside world? If they cannot help you, try to recollect your most early days before the conditional world ensnared you in its restrictive bind. Maybe you were a collector, maybe puzzles fascinated you, maybe it was exploring toys by first destroying them, maybe dancing or singing, maybe cycling into the sunset, painting, writing, playing with sand, it could be as obscure as possible. But what were those hobbies and interests that you were glued to and pestered your parents about?

Why am I insisting so much on immersions? Well, I believe that when so much of you can be devoted to the external world, maybe you owe it to yourself to immerse a small part of you in yourself. We all need something more than those around us, no matter how close and supportive, to feel like ours—that small legacy we can leave behind. So, find or further invest in that immersion, which is your true witness to the time spent on Earth.

What fascinates you? I give you my list below, and feel free to add yours to it.

- Writing (duh!)
- Occult—exploring the mysterious.
- Long road trips in a sturdy 4-wheeler driven by me obviously.
- Travel to new and remote lands (but no camping please!)
- Learning Italian, Spanish, or Portuguese, whichever is easier.
- Understanding and discovering Latin.
- Mythology of the European lands.

#3

Are we anchored?

We search and hold on to our anchors pretty much throughout our lives. What are anchors? I define them as things, emotions, patterns, or relationships that you hold on to, as steady and strong supports, with the belief that they bring you stability. Most of the times, these anchors are outside of us as we desperately seek something or someone who will not change with changing times.

While I am on my sea analogy, the problem is that the ports we place our anchors on, keep changing. Also, the boats that we are riding constantly seek new directions and may even collapse by the loads, wear and tears, and long journeys.

So, we create anew. We build new boats, find new ports, and cast new anchors. Not an easy task. Sometimes you just want things to be stationary, to not keep changing so unpredictably. Perhaps you are not questioning the status quo, but if you are a traveller or a soul-seeker, who is constantly needing to evolve and grow, then anchors are also going to change.

As your "boat" of life, changes directions, as the growth-impelled soul begs for new shores, how can the anchors stay the same? That job you have been hanging on to for years if not decades, that bank balance you have been steadily building towards retirement, that spouse, that parent/s, that son/daughter, that house, that country, that friend/s; all or at least some of these will be tested or forced to change too. So, what do we do then? When we find that our anchors have been moved, released, or removed from our lives by will or circumstances. What do we do then? Do we find new anchors? Do we change boats and keep living with this sense of search and seeking inside of us?

Or do we realise, practically and spiritually, that the real anchors have been a small, limited set of relationships in the deeply satisfying internal world. Our daily endeavours to keep ourselves and our precious relationships healthy and steady have been the real anchors. *Our efforts are our true anchors.*

REMEDIES

While I am definitely not talking of therapeutic or medicinal remedies, I am definitely talking about remedies to make this life stage so euphoric, you spin like a dervish.

#1

Joie de vivre

Do you remember when was the last time your heart pounded with excitement? When you felt truly alive, when you felt like flying, and when you last screamed out aloud in joy? Remember zest? Remember youthfulness? Remember adventure? No? Then you are in deep trouble.

Yes, the body says you are middle-aged, the mirror confirms it, but the spirit, the heart says—I have miles to go before I sleep. Are we being delusional when we say this? Not really, there are many men and women around who want to revive their *joie de vivre* and pulsate with vivaciousness or are already doing it. Refusing to accept that age and spirit are correlated, they co-create life with hobbies, interests, travelling, adventures (including extreme), and pretty much anything that makes the blood surge. And some can do that alongside work too—yes this does happen even now

Joie de vivre is defined as "the exuberant enjoyment of life" and need not translate to a tangible, physical response. It could also be a sense of quiet happiness emanating from peace, a loving companionship or loving familial moments. It could be a hammock, cuppa coffee, books, music—pretty much anything that sends you vibrating upwards.

The mirror possibly becomes our worst enemy, and the well-dressed youth do not help, nor does a society obsessed with looking younger. Discussing health, girth, diminishing stamina, and speed while secretly envying those who are able to retain robust levels does not help either. It is natural that the middle-aged will look a little, well, *cough* "experienced" against the rosy glow of the nubile and visit the dermatologists/ cosmetic surgeons more often. But here is the thing, if this helps you sprint towards your personal joie de vivre, then by all means indulge. However, if this is leading to more envy, more trips to the mirror, and intense scrutiny, then this is definitely a downward spiral.

Start a support group, question what the society dictates, wear what you can carry off confidently, and for heaven's sake, if that tightly belted dress is going to kill your joy, burn it. Strong words, but I mean them.

I am starting a support group to bring Joie de vivre back into the middle-aged's life. Only three rules in this support group called "Joie" (for ease of remembering):

1. No conversations around health anxieties and that includes weight gains, skin rejuvenation, etc.
2. No conversations around the approaching elderly ages including who will look after us, where will we live, etc.
3. No conversations around work, politics, money, business, expenses, etc.

So how do we attain this near *euphoric* state? Read on…

#2

Staying inspired for Joie de vivre …

THOSE days when you wake up refreshed, jumping out of bed, ready to charge for the day ahead…. Wait… huh? Let me jog my memory to see when it last happened. Oh yes, it happened on the days I could look forward to something fun, recreational, like travel or social events—so those are my sources of inspiration. What are yours?

A lot many things and people inspire you when you are young, when you are still exploring and still finding new terrains, ideas, learnings, etc. As you reach middle-age and beyond, inspiration has to be hunted for. It has to be searched for under rocks, behind the trees, in the shadows of your mind, and in the foothills of the mountains to be climbed. You get the picture, right? It is not going to be as readily available as it was before.

Yet inspiration is the single most important driver for everyday living and indeed, thriving. The opposite of inspiration is languishing, and that, to my mind, is one of the most vampiric states to be in. While inspiration lifts, languishing drains. When you are inspired, everything feels possible, all dreams seem within reach and the sky beckons.

Artists look for muses, for inspiration because after a while even the act of creation may not be enough—the subject too is important. As is oft said, artists are temperamental creatures. What on earth does that mean? My interpretation is that when artists lack inspiration, they, well, languish, and their unpredictability comes from this state.

Indeed, only saints and very evolved souls can consistently seek inspiration from within. However, at times when there are no muses, no external stimuli, it may help to truly see what hidden potential lies within us and see if we can again be inspired by things/ideas we had pushed into the deep crevices of our subconscious. Any new skill you wanted to learn—language, skill, art, cooking, sport, video game, etc.?

Last but not the least, for heaven's sake, reach out and make new friends. Do not be so selective that you are left alone, which can happen very easily in the middle-ages. That jaded, cynical person can completely take over and kill inspiration—hence it is important to find people and ask what inspires them. Equally. You owe it to them to walk the talk of inspiration. You never know who strikes that inspiration, and that will wake you up with a jaunty spring to your step.

#3

The balancing act

BY the middle-ages you have realised, released with a sigh, that life has been and will be, an amalgamation of the mundane and the inspiring. Since you have lived, imbibed, and dealt superbly with the mundane during your earlier years, when you had the zest and hope for it, the mundane settles down to being second nature to you. Now you can go riding into the sunset in search for the inspirational. Hurrah! you found it—rejoice, for it is not everyone who at the age of 45–50 still finds something to be inspired by.

Apologies in advance for what I am about to say—here is the bummer—you realise that while you would like to dedicate yourself to your inspiration now, it is still new, and you may still be learning or it may be out of reach as yet due to multiple reasons. However, if the pull is strong, you will be determined to go through this. Fear not, the mundane always comes to your rescue.

How can I say that? Well, history is replete with instances where struggling writers, artisans, etc., filled their stomachs and fuelled their kitchen fires with the mundane and reserved their creative, obsessively guarded passion for their inspiration. In these modern days, alas, where there are no patrons for the artisans, the mundane comes to their rescue like a knight in shining armour. In your experienced years of being a seasoned professional, you can now conduct the mundane with a flick of your wrist. Yet another relieving aspect of being middle-aged.

As you excitedly work on your inspiration, akin to the mischievous child indulging their late-night reading under the torch-lit tent, hidden from prying parents, zealously bringing it to life. Be happy that the mundane keeps the rest of your responsibilities at bay. You know now how to attend those laborious meetings with a half-mind, make decisions based on intuitive learnings and experience and attend to deliverables with a smooth mentorship crafted by years in the dungeon of work.

In short, rather than resenting the mundane, celebrate your daily work routine or whatever you have been doing for a living, the fire kept alive by your inspiration. While balancing the mundane and the inspiring, do aim for that one miraculous day where your inspiration is all that you will be doing.

#4

Be kind to yourself and others

COMPASSION is the reward gained by the middle-aged. So how do we really define it?

- Is it listening interspersed with empathetic nodding or sounds of agreement?
- Is it feeling sorry about the person's situation and the person,
- Or is it giving advice or solutions?

I define compassion as a little mixture of all of these elements, but most importantly, knowing in your middle-ages that you may also have the resources to help out the person.

By this time, we have learnt and understood that *cooperation, collaboration,* and *communication* are the three most important cornerstones to success. We have also understood that patience, persistence, and practicality (practical is not the anti-thesis of dreaming but having realistic plans to fulfil them), are the three pillars of strength. This combination of external stimuli—success—and internal core strength, creates wisdom, opportunities, and the ability to help others. This is the way I would define compassion—having not only wisdom and empathy, but also the means to help others.

Yet many of the privileged, and I do not define privileged as having healthy bank accounts and assets, but anyone who can provide the smallest of opportunities or help to others, will listen actively. They will even be empathetic and wise, but will stop short of being truly compassionate. I have honestly always pondered at that thought. What stops those on a rising curve of life from lending a hand to the person at the descent of the curve?

It is all very simple, really. If the universe has been kind enough to reward all your hard work and arduous labour with riches, success, and health, could it be that this happened so you could do the same for others? If you can back your advice with some actual help, a lending hand, even if it is as small as a referral, pointing to the right opportunity, providing the contact of that right person, or calling up that potential investor, etc., *this is compassion.*

Any emotional support without any physical evidence of support, however small or meagre, is empathy. Not to say empathy is not needed or unimportant, but when you are in the middle of your adult life, surely you can extend yourself a little more.

Where I am reaching with all this rhetoric is that middle-ages are a crossroad—that juncture in your life to look back and look ahead, simultaneously. How, and with what perspective, you look back and look ahead is what makes midlife a place of crisis or a place of satisfaction. Once you have purged all the so-called failures of your past years, you start seeing what all you have gained and how far you have really come.

The midlife, for me, was a turning point to realise that there are many compassionate acts to offer—teaching, healing, networking for others, bridging the needs of the youth with the access of the experienced, lending monetary and physical help where one could safely do, intervening where needed, and providing opportunities. Despite this, I feel inadequate and unable to help many who come my way and I try to ask middle-aged peers to help them. It is painful to see that not many carry a compassionate streak, for they are themselves caught in a poverty-stricken mindset.

The poverty-stricken mindset has little to do with actual bank balance and assets owned. It is an attitude or confidence with which you approach life. If you are in a state of constant insecurity, you look back and see only failures and struggles and how uphill life has been. You will never feel satisfied or grateful, and will hoard your connections, your network, your resources, including your emotional availability, just in case you need these one day for yourself or your kin. Some call it thriftiness; I call it hoarding.

Compassion does not mean that you squander all your resources, or overexert to the point of your own exhaustion, but what it does mean is coming from a mindset of abundance. It does mean assessing what and how much one can help others without being over-leveraged. It does mean actively and seriously considering every cry of help to see what can be done tangibly to bring the person out of this situation.

#5

Stay humble with self-deprecating humour

I FEEL the British (sorry again for using stereotypes) are perpetually in a state of being middle-aged, if the TV shows are to be believed. They seem to have conquered and mastered self-deprecating humour. It is a wonderful strategy when things go downhill, which happens a little more than wanted.

Dry wit, light-hearted sarcastic humour at one's own expense and admitting to mistakes in a non-judgmental way are some powerful ways of coping with the travesties of daily living. Self-deprecating humour is basically used to make fun of yourself, anticipating that others will do it otherwise.

Take this fun quotient away and you wouldn't know how to get out of the treacherously addictive pull of self-pity. At any time that you become a victim of it, rather than finding unsuspecting souls to exhaust, try this trick. Convert the self-pity into a self-deprecating statement dripping with dry wit and then call friends to share. This way, they laugh at what they perceive as a joke, and you get to vent. Good ploy, right?

Vast generalisations and projections to other humans are also coping mechanisms as you scramble to suggest that you are not the only one who could possibly be suffering, there must be many going through the same. You generalise about men, women, or children and so on, as that makes it easier to rationalise the behaviour of near and dear ones.

If it helps, by all means use these techniques, but here is the caution—do not start believing them. Understand that these are coping techniques and tread lightly on these waters knowing that these are not your truths. *Capisce*?

#6

Drift away! You've earned it!

DRIFTING aimlessly in the valleys of the mind, there are days when you just want to do nothing. No aims, no productivity, no goals, no conversations, just the need to be seated on a cloud that keeps moving, controlled by an unpredictable gust of air. Replete in itself, the cloud seeks no protection, has no fears when surrendering itself to the mercies of the wind and the sky.

After trying to control your life through youth and much of the middle ages, you realise how peaceful surrender is. I admit it is occasional, but what a relief. Hopefully, you have reached that stage in life where you don't have to respond to office calls or emails on a Sunday, you don't need to do anything you don't want to do, and like the clouds, you too have earned your drifting time.

Does that sound like retirement? The only difference between the surrender of the middle-aged and the surrender of retirement is that middle-ages give you a sabbatical—a pause to surrender occasionally. It is an intermittent experience, while the surrender of retirement is almost inevitable, an external push unless you put plans to resist it.

After endlessly chasing some target, milestone, or position, mostly enforced by the rat race, you surrender to the middle-aged possibility that maybe now you can take your eyes off the ball and relax a little. Or at least till the next restless urge to reach a higher goal catches up and bites you.

The surrender of the middle-aged feels particularly sweet as it tastes almost like the forbidden fruit. You feel guilty taking that time and surrendering to whatever mood washes over you—relaxing, travelling, doing nothing on a hammock, or any such non-active stuff. The list of pending activities, work, and other chores drill into your brain, prodding you to jump out of that state of lassitude. But till that happens, you sigh pleasurably and say, "Everything can wait awhile."

PART THREE

ACTIONS

Get your mojo back

1

Become your own storyteller

To cope with these problems, we spin yarns of stories every day, telling ourselves and other people many untruths, mostly based on truths. We convince ourselves so very well that the story may as well become our real life. This is a good thing if the storyteller and the protagonist merge harmoniously, and the narrative is hopeful and upbeat. But if this is not so, then it can have very unhappy consequences.

So, be careful about the words you speak about yourself, not only in front of others but also to yourself in the bathroom mirror, standing stark naked as the day you were born. That, my friend, is the real you. As you approach middle-age, that picture in the mirror may not be very pleasant and it will show strains of a body well-used. Yet you can choose to see it as a mere visual, or you could choose to see the incredible journey of life with all its major and minor storytelling moments, nested in each cell of your body. So, I repeat, chose the story, the storytelling device, the crescendos, and the valleys of your story incredibly carefully.

Borrowing from an article I read, written by Marguerite Theophil for *Times of India*, she says "To begin re-storying and, thus, restoring your life, "reshape" your narrative. First stop blaming yourself, the circumstances or others. Take time to figure out who you truly are—your gifts and failings. What behaviours need to change? How do you want to be in the future? What baby steps can you initiate for these changes to take shape?"

If you are indeed unhappy with your life story thus far, ask yourself—what in heaven's name is stopping you from changing it? Who is stopping you? Is it the family, the neighbours, your friends, your occupation, or job? Or maybe, just maybe, is it you alone?

But even more important than this questioning is to ask yourself honestly, what is the new storyline or narrative that you want to create for yourself. Who do you want to be titled as? What byline under your name do you want the world to see, and lastly, what storyline protagonist makes you feel that this indeed is you and your skin?

By all means, go ahead and plan this new avatar, this new role and script, hopefully, with minimal collateral damage. Better to aim for a simple novella than a dragging saga of eternal dramas. What do you say?

- In a story, there is a broad plot, divided into chapters that carry through from start to end.
- There is an arch—subplots of happenings that curve up and lead to the climax, descend towards the anticlimax, and finally the conclusion.
- You can create this story, the chapters, and the climax, which is a discomfort that this will inevitably happen to you and others, and the corrective measures you will take

to comfort yourself and others towards the anticlimax, which, hopefully, is the new self that you resurrected.

This is how a story flows, with many meanderings, lost paths, and painful rocks along the way. A word of caution—the story should not be re-written because you are bored. There has to be a significant reason, and should neither be a kneejerk reaction or reactive state of mind. The calmer, more self-contained, and more accepting you are of your current status quo, the better and more enriched will be the new or revised story.

Ultimately you are the author of your life's story and would it not be better to make it a book of happy endings?

2

Storytellers (Part 2)

ONE of my favourite past times is to coax fellow middle-aged to reveal their interesting twists and turns. You can be absolutely sure of one thing—by this time, most would have at least one or two jolts, sudden developments, providential highs, and despairing lows.

As we exchanged these twists like veterans discussing war stories, we felt proud of our peers' battles and wins. As wisdom reveals that success comes with scars, hence admiration is more relevant than envy.

We learn how some have scraped rock bottom, losing millions in business, betrayals, or incorrect investments, yet ploughed their way back up. We learn about how some have early health problems and how their body fought back. We learn of homes destroyed by earthquakes and their brick by brick resurrection. Their stories of sniffing out new opportunities with twice the determination are truly uplifting.

All in all, these occurrences become stories for close-knit cozy dinners in a safe, non-judgmental environment.

3

Face It, Diagnose It, and then Release It

HERE is a corollary to being a storyteller. Now that I have handled all of us with kid gloves, gently and amicably, let me take us through a more hard-hitting version of the same. I can understand this may not be everyone's cup of tea, so I completely condone you skipping this piece.

Conversing with fellow travellers on this journey to the middle-ages, I have noticed that some have come through unscathed, with intact personas and pretty much the same personality that they had in their heydays. Then there are others, who have this bizarre need to constantly scrutinise and create or react to circumstances that shake them to their core. Scarred, shaken, stirred—James Bond would completely understand the end result. However, unlike James Bond, who emerges heroic and confident after all the shakes and stirs, we are not as lucky.

On this journey, we would have made colossal mistakes, and caused intentional and unintentional harm or hurt to others and self. The trick is to reveal all of these to yourself as reflections in front of the mirror, without justifying, rationalising, or even giving yourself an escape route. Sounds harsh and unnecessary? Not really, actually it is very easy if you can do it without getting emotionally involved with it. After all, we do it to others almost all the time—judging, opining, and advising without truly understanding them or their situations. So why would we not be able to do that to ourselves?

When this honest scrutiny is happening, it is important to approach from a position of self-awareness and not self-criticism—to know why you are doing this scrutiny and what would be the end use of it. Like I said, it is not for the fainthearted and there are reasons why it happens in the middle-ages and not earlier.

One, in our heydays we were blissfully unaware, too caught up in life and strutting in our comfortable sense of invincibility. Two, the scars and wounds are still being treated and we chose easy reasons for their explanation. It is only now, when we have crossed that bridge, that we can look back and start reacting. If you are continuing with the same patterns and mistakes even in this stage of your life, then that naked scrutiny is imperative.

Why should we do it? Why not just accept all the praise and validation from others for our goodness and positivity and be happy? Well, all that is great, but is not as real as this. Despite the light and the shining parts of us, do take out the time to unearth and shine the light on the duality in us—that side which is as much a part of us as the good parts. Bring them out, scrutinise them, understand them and resolve them… just don't suppress them. Then and only then will you truly become a storyteller of your life and change the ending.

How about a little tough love?

- What are the patterns you notice and want to discard?
- What do you hide from the world ?
- What mistakes do not bear repeating?
- What dark spaces need some sunshine?

4

Rediscovery

WHILE you are shining light on parts not exposed to the sun. Ah no, I don't mean your body parts, I mean the hidden, shyer parts of your personality. Brush aside the uncertainties and see if it helps uncover your mysteries by….

- Travelling solo
- Meeting people who are not from your community or country
- Going for events, places alone, where you know no one
- Eating solo, going for movies alone
- Learning a new language
- Making friends with the international communities
- Joining clubs, hobby groups
- Travelling with strangers

The above is just a glimpse of things you can do to discover parts of yourself even you didn't know of. You discover how the limelight is never about comfort and almost always about crawling out of your skin. Embrace this, for the rewards are immense.

5

Please Do Me a Favour, Get Out of Your Way!

CAN'T you see, you are the single biggest obstacle to your own success. You might find references to it in some books—it is called fear of success. Aah, now it clicks into place, right? Yes, we do stand in our way as we want to control success too.

We are afraid of not being successful and we are afraid of being successful—how paradoxical we human beings are. At the first chance of success, we are smug and say, "see, I knew this would work" and at the first glitch of failure, "see I knew this would not work." Both ways, you are in the way. Neither does something succeed without glitches and neither does failure happen without moments of success. It is truly what you want to chase and persist with. Things fail because we lose interest—this can happen in a domino effect when one wrong move cascades to several losses.

That means you have to give yourself permission—permission to start afresh, think laterally, try other routes, or even go back to the basics and resurrect, both professionally and personally. It was never about the idea, the person, or the job. It is always about how well you receive it, how much you want it despite problems and your will power wants to see it through. I know, feels exhausting, right?

Yet, the solution is simple, you are exhausted because you are fighting and are in conflict within yourself. The outside world does not tire you, your internal demons, insecurities, over-thinking fearful mind tires you. Stop the cross-questioning and self-recrimination, stop criticising yourself (and your loved ones), thinking if I criticise myself, others will not.

It is not about self-criticism but being honest with yourself. Honesty means having a personal balance sheet of your strengths (assets) and weaknesses (liabilities). Increase the value of your strengths and decrease the value of your liabilities so that the profit (your productive self) becomes high.

Remove your doubting hind from the road of success and zip your way through.

6

Ask for Help!

MIDDLE age is a tough era because you, your family, and your children expect you to have reached a pinnacle of success, and most of us do. However, that definition of success differs from family to family.

Mistakes become costly in more than one way and risks are frowned upon, as there are so many dependents.

No family member, adolescent child or elderly parent, can or should expect the middle-aged member to be perfect, in complete control, and steadfast. Along with meeting the expectations of the outside world, their inner world too needs attention—sandwiched as they are between external and internal worlds.

In this pull and push, they may falter and stumble, and for a short while fall from the pedestal their family has placed them on. In striving to reach success, the edge might be where things fail, and they too need the world around them to pause their judgments at that time.

It may take one middle-aged person to help the other. Peers and same-aged friends might come more to your rescue than family. Take all the help you can as you balance the need to fulfil duties and your own dreams. You may reach a point where chasing the proverbial rainbow might draw you away from the routine, where the exhaustion of showing up for others may be too much, and responsibilities may make you feel overwhelmed. All your wisdom, strength, and perspective may not help. Feel free to reach out and not assume that you have it all under control.

You know what, do this right away, pick up the phone and thank that person who has always had your back.

7

Gamble

"I FIGURE you have the same chance of winning the lottery whether you play or not."

~Fran Lebowitz

You tried, you failed, you tried again, and you failed again. Yet you stand up, ready to gamble on yourself again. The only question you ask yourself—how badly do I want this. What exactly is "this"? It could be anything—a new venture, a new job, a new or renewed hobby, etc. Like any gamble, what it might entail is some trade-offs.

There is a difference between trade-offs and compromises; one does not mean the other. Trade-offs are the way of evaluating and making choices that work for you. You may change the dynamics of something and accept it as a necessary aspect of living. Therin lies the gamble, when you traded-off between choices.

Some of us may object to the word gambling, but if you were to think about it a bit, have we not gambled on ourselves thus far? Barring the lucky few who inherit a business, and even among them, we gambled when we decided what college or course to pursue. We gambled when we took our first job and we gambled when we decided to marry. Life really doesn't come with guarantees and we clutch at apparent stable pillars, hoping to row our boat of life safely to the shore.

As we all know and have experienced, those so-called stable pillars crumble at a moment's notice. There is a limit to which the future can be predicted through excel sheets, simulation exercises, or even consulting your family astrologer. Ultimately, that leap of faith needs to be taken, well, with a leap. I am not sure why we look for mountains to climb or leap from, but from experience one knows that growth, momentum, and learnings have not really come from allowing the fungus to grow under a comfort rock.

Big or small, giving sustenance or abundance, these are not as much in question as in the will to step out of the comfort zone and create something. It could either be a retirement plan or better still a legacy to be left behind for the future generation.

Calculate the odds, measure the risks, find the right "casino" for your business idea. Do all the homework you want, but know this—it is still a gamble, and as any gambler would say—win or lose, the chances are 50:50.

- ✎ What terrifies you?
- ✎ What discomforts you?
- ✎ What feels like the leap into the unknown?

8

Overhauling Ourselves

ENGINE of cars frequently need overhauling—batteries, soot, mud, wires, brakes, accelerators, all need repair—to function. Well, we are no different. Our engines need overhauling too and they frequently break down, around this age. I don't mean just the physical engine of our body, but more importantly, the mental engine—the real fuel to our acceleration.

Every once in a while, open the hood of your mind, just as you would for your car, to see what is malfunctioning. Examine the crisscrossed wires, brush off any dust, the leftover decayed material of yesteryears. Clean the black soot off the batteries, recharge them with fresh fuel, fill the emptied pipes with fresh, clean water, and wipe the parts till they sparkle clean.

Create gaps by removing muck so new energy can rush in. Do not underestimate the amount of clutter you can accumulate in your brain. We are living in very polluted surroundings and just as your car has gaps through which dirt seeps in and settles, so does our mind. Filter the thoughts, opinions, and conversations around you so only freshness seeps in through the gaps. Imagine a sparkling-white mind filled with oxygen and clean fuel. Imagine the acceleration, the smoothness, and the direction with which it will travel.

The next time you take your car for a service or an overhaul, maybe you should accompany it and replicate the actions for self.

9

Make that Bucket List

SUDDENLY that bucket list is no longer a term you read somewhere or saw in a movie. It feels real, looming like a shadow around you, and you start conjuring one. Maybe it comprises of all those ideas you felt too scared to explore. I am sure one of the items would be travelling to exotic, adventurous, soulful places. Maybe there is a craft, a creative pursuit, or a list of books or movies that you wanted to see. Was it deep-sea diving, zip-line crossing, or skydiving that you wanted to try?

Whatever may be the items in your list, do consider doing it, and also a suggestion from me, if I may. Do include making new friends, visiting relatives or friends who maybe live far away, and exploring new relationships as parts of this bucket list. Try not to make the list only an *acquisition*s list again. I mean, we have acquired many materialistic pleasures and things in our life, so do we really want our bucket list also to be a competitive race, a tick mark of those exotic adventures alone that we could boast about? At the end, the bucket list is more about the things missing from our lives that we want to experience. So we can reminiscence when we are old and foggy-brained.

Let the bucket list be about curiosity. What are those people, things, places, and pursuits that you are still curious about? What are the new learnings, knowledge, memories, values, or perceptions that you can gather to add to the portfolio of life?

Another important instruction, and this is really an order, not a suggestion—make that bucket list happen. Write it and honour it. It may not be completed in on go—you need a lot of time for that, but start with tackling the hard ones—you know, the ones that need stamina, rugged strength, focus, etc., while you still can! Leave the slower, gentler ones for later.

Also, again honour the bucket list by having a witness—maybe a like-minded friend, sibling, your child, spouse/partner, etc.—whoever is interested and invested in you and can be sure to motivate and push you towards your bucket. Sometimes, we become overly serious about ourselves, about our lives, and the bucket list becomes a frivolous, impulsive embarrassment. Do not consider it one. Actually, it is what gives you purpose, what motivates you towards upholding a mundane, work-oriented routine, and most importantly, shows that there are new discoveries ahead. Go write it down!

My bucket list consists of :

✎ ....

✎ ....

✎ ....

✎ ....

✎ ....

10

Be a Little Annoying

Go ahead, be a little annoying, you deserve it. If you are feeling like a neglected, toiling, and thankless member of your society, go ahead and voice your complaints. Surely, you deserve it after 25–30 years of a blemish-free existence since the dawn of adulthood.

Some of us chose to be annoying by going against the tide. In that respect, we may become a source of discomfort to our immediate family and friends. Many of us run into marital issues, divorces, financial issues, work issues, health issues, or at the very least, an acute case of boredom.

We may start indulging in goofier behaviour, hobbies, and interests that are meaningless except for their entertainment and comfortable presence. To that extent, we may become annoyingly embarrassing for our family and grown-up children.

As you go about re-discovering yourself behind the veil of life, you may find yourself awash with many innovative ideas and dreams. Before the inner critic surfaces, quickly zone in on a few and get started. I know how maddening it can be for grown-up children and family to see their almost elderly parents experimenting, so keep it under wraps initially.

If people around you get provoked or single you out for being an eyesore in their perfect world, perfect home, and perfect charades, so be it. Continue being your annoying self that rejects the mundane because secretly the conventional are actually inspired by your annoyances.

11

Don't Stop Asking, "Why?"

As children, we are curious about everything and persist with questions till we receive satisfactory answers.

Alas, we grew up. We stopped asking as we think we have figured it all out.

Sometimes it takes hard jolts of life to shake us up from adult lethargy and comfort. We are backed into corners like wounded animals with no choice but to survive. In a more positive vein, what we think are setbacks may instead be opportunities to reinvent and take further risks. It brings us back to that same word with which we started life—why! We wonder *why* this happened to me, *why* is it not correcting itself, *why* does this keep repeating, etc. And just like that, we become children again.

As teenagers, we did silly things like staying awake the whole night just to see what it feels like to challenge sleep. Or we rebelled against the rules of attendance and did a "mass-bunk" (as it used to be called in my circles), just to see how the school reacts. While conducting lab experiments, we ascertained how tiny changes can create explosive outcomes; the learning years were full of fun, exploration, and excitement. Life was still unfolding and there was so much more to know.

As we enter middle-ages, we assume we have all the answers. Some of us may even declare ourselves as experts, though the recipients of our ponderous outpourings may call us a pompous know-it-all. We are genuinely experts or at least deeply knowledgeable in certain fields by this age, but that gives us no right to extend that label to all aspects of life.

Playtime is the white space for children where they break things, mess up, and use different materials just to satisfy their innate curiosity and the question of why does this happen? Anyone, and more so the sedate, comfortable middle-aged, has to extend, surprise, and even threaten themselves so that they have yet another why answered. Do try to upset the apple cart—at the very least, a new answer will reveal itself.

✎ What assumptions in your life would you like to question?

12

Prioritise Yourself

MOST of us put so much energy into taking care of others that prioritising our own needs can feel downright foreign and uncomfortable.

We have a wonderful capacity for making pain recede to a corner of our hearts or brains so that it becomes more tolerable. Occasional bouts of nostalgia apart, we soon busy ourselves in the routine of the day, start paying more attention to those around us, and are happy to keep tightening the circle of relationships till it is brought down to a significant few. And then the day arrives when there are not too many in our midst, and we suddenly wake up and wonder, "God, where is everybody?"

Like a Lazarus being reborn from a grave, we need to rebirth.

As people come and go, and even as we miss others, do take out the time to look after yourself, and prioritise your needs and welfare. In this midst of comings and goings, you are that stationary, solid core that stands strong.

Thereafter, once stable again, there are several options available to cope—you can become practical and realistic about people going, or be a soddy grieving mess of emotions, or an emotional fool for whom relationships may be their biggest investments. Being an emotional sod does make life a little difficult and inconvenient but then what else is life's purpose but to build legacies through relationships? To modify the famous book title, not *Who will cry when you die* but rather "Who will cry with you when you are alive?"

- ✎ What parts of you feel neglected and are yearning for self-care, me-time, self-love?
- ✎ What aspects of your life need some emotional boundaries?

13

Stop Playing the Blame Game

YES, it is completely a game—a delusional game we play with others and ourselves. It is never about us; it is always about the other, the external.

Blame is a way of bringing logic or rational thinking into a situation which does not always feel right. Since we are conditioned to be logical beings, rather than intuitive beings, just the fact that our heart is not in something or if we are feeling unsuited, uncared for are not enough reasons. So, we find rationalisations, we find the faults in the situation, the person, or in the work to justify our feelings.

Ironically, we never need to justify good feelings, good happenings, or creditable situations/people. Yet bad feelings or discomfort need justifications. When did this happen? And more importantly, why do we need to play this game with ourselves?

The job, the person, the place, or the relationship does not feel right? Go ahead and admit that feeling to yourself honestly instead of trying to find faults. Here is the real deal—if you are on a fault-finding mission or in the quest for perfection, you are headed for self-sabotage. You will find something missing or wrong and will rationalise yourself out of that situation, place, job, or relationship. Of course, there are times when we are wronged unfairly, hurt, or harmed—these are obvious situations to get out of and place blame rightfully.

However, it must be understood that people will be unpredictable, critical, or imperfect, and hence blame will be an ongoing, never-ending journey that can never find a destination. If you are blaming a workplace, stop and consider if you are unhappy with the people, your own performance, or if you are not enjoying your work anymore. The latter is the only authentic feeling. The rest is a blame game again. If a line of work is not up your alley, you will not enjoy it even if you are doing it alone and have no one to blame.

If you are feeling bored, irritated, or stagnant in a place or relationship, acknowledge that feeling and assess what in *you* has created that feeling, more so than others. What can you do differently? What new perspectives can you acquire? How can you distract yourself? What newness can you bring into you or your life? Does examining the situation from another's point of view or detaching emotionally from it give better perspectives? Examine the feelings and then discover the cause.

Blaming others is like jumping into the deep sea without a lifejacket. You will drown and you alone are responsible for it. Harsh words, but hey, I need someone to blame too!

14

Be a Lucid Dreamer

WHAT is the difference between a lucid dreamer and a daydreamer? Well, the latter dreams to escape reality and the former dreams to make the reality a little dreamlike. Both are visionaries and entitled to their fantasies, but there is a tad more sense to the lucid dreamer.

Being a voracious and hopelessly addicted daydreamer, I have faced the excruciating disappointments of not having them fulfilled. It took me till middle-age to understand why most of my daydreams just ended up in the dustbin, or if they did materialise, they could not stand the tangible test of time. The list below also helps explain what makes a daydream convert into a lucid dream and ultimately into a dreamlike reality.

1. You cannot daydream on the shoulders of someone else. What this means is that you cannot expect others to be equally enthused about your daydream and make the sacrifices you are willing to make. So, while they may promote, invest, push along, they may not understand or share that instinctive fervour that keeps you going.

Hence, lucid dreaming can only materialise if it is dependent mostly on you.

2. It has to fall somewhere within in the realms of possibility. I do not mean it cannot be innovative, visionary, or even unrealistic, but there should be some starting points that allow tangibility to take over.
3. The dreams can't be so difficult that night sets in before the journey is halfway over. What I mean is that the dream's destination is to make reality dreamlike and not a void that cannot be filled.
4. If the daydream can incorporate a few instances of "what is the worst that can happen" and you have the answers and can ride the bumps, then it has the potential of a lucid dream.
5. Last but not the least, your dream should not make you feel shy, embarrassed, or hesitant—you should be so engaged and passionate about it that it supersedes all these inhibitions, and you are like a possessed-person.

VISION BOARD

15

Lyrics and Salsa

WITH these, we can express with mirthful abandon—sing like there is no audience and dance like there is no rhythm. Caught in the perfections of art and artists, we have forgotten the charm of spontaneous expression. When we dance or sing to our heart's content, we move beyond the banalities of the everyday towards the thin ledge of joyful ridicule.

If you want to spare the family and neighbours and not bray in the bathroom, then write some beautiful lyrics, if that is not your forte then express through poems. If that too terrifies you, then enjoy the musical waves surrounding your room through the open window.

Dancing is singularly the best cardio you could enliven your liver with. Huh...heart or liver? I believe pumping the liver is even better than the heart in terms of making you happy. Or better still dance so hard, after checking the sturdiness of the wooden floors and the thickness of the curtains, that every part of the body is pumped. Learn Salsa, Kathak, Flamenco, Waltz,

Belly Dance (that would also help your burgeoning tummy), anything that inspires movement and pleasure.

I have known many who stepped out of their closets and are not only performing but are also opening centres of excellence—teaching and expressing. What could be better?

16

Be Silent, Be Nice

ON a related note, you will find that people who stay within the grey zone use *silence* and *niceness* effectively.

These are also two words that are often misconstrued and neglected. In the current world, surrounded by a cacophony of noises, loud voices demanding their opinions be heard and recognised, silence is indeed golden. It is true that wisdom lies in silent contemplation and then speaking thoughts that are well, nice.

There is a direct correlation between silence, deep introspection, and verbalising niceness. The first thoughts/reactions may actually be more harmful, as they can tend to be judgmental and an absorption of societal behaviour and thought processes. However, speaking after the reaction time has passed and the second thoughts/paused reactions bubble up, those would probably come from a place of wisdom or at least are nicer.

It is also important to understand that nice people will value the relationship more than having the last word, will value keeping the bond peaceful more than creating arguments that finally have not much consequence. Niceness is also displayed through kindness—understanding the battles of the other person and being kind enough not to add to these battles. Silence from nice people emanates not from agreement necessarily, but from the tolerance that differing opinions are not more important than the person.

However, there are times that even niceness has to be left aside, much to the chagrin of the person, for larger themes of peace, assertion, and self-defence. This happens to inform others that niceness does not indicate weakness, softness or allowing domination.

Niceness comes from a place of self-containment. In turn, self-containment comes from a high sense of personal power. Nice people are quite confident in their own sense of power and do not need to yield control or power over others. They operate from self-love and hence the need to love others as well. They may not ask or expect much from others as their needs are being met by own self. The only advice to nice people is to not be so silent at crucial times as sometimes the world needs to hear their quiet loving voice and opinions more than the strident calls of those with afflicted egos.

Nice people are also not ignorant of the ways of the world. They do understand that gentleness can allow intimidation from others, that softness of opinions and voice can allow abrasive sounds, and peace can be misconstrued as grounds for domination. Innate intelligence is what leads to a person adopting niceness over all other emotions, he/she empathises and understands the internal battles of those who chose power over collaboration.

In the end, nice people do not finish last, they just try to time action and emotions, so that they can have the last word—since actions and words emitting from a place of self-assurance will always prove others wrong. Action based on consensus and collaboration is the mantra of nice people and this always has a long-lasting impact.

17

Change the Terra Firma

QUITE a few of my middle-aged friends have shifted gears. Some have moved countries or are in the process, discovering new interests along the way. A few have gone to more peaceful, less-crowded cities within the country.

Many that I know are contemplating shaking their very roots—to whichever country suits their middle-aged energies. Even while planning, they wonder, "Which country is better and how will we emerge, where to spend years post the mid-years, or where will we feel sustained," and many more such thoughts. Even as they ponder, they move towards actioning their plans.

Why do they shift their terra firma? It is probably a mixture of many reasons—boredom, stagnation, better infrastructure, weather conditions, nature, work opportunities, cost of living, closer to children, etc. Sometimes it could be as simple as current city or country being less palatable and, thus, evaluating a few trade-offs.

Ultimately, it is about finding your own peaceful corner in some part of the world and staying true to it. If your loved ones are around and can nurture you, you are blessed. As you move into your new ground, the outside world exerts lower levels of influence and any journeys made to find your living place is mostly balancing your energies with that of the geographical location.

People are contradictory and so are countries. Which is a better country to live in is a rhetoric question really, for our energies keep shifting and responding to the pull of different shores. Speaking for myself, I have always been a traveller and a seeker, so to anchor, I do not need the welcome of an entire country or community, just the welcoming hands of a few.

For those of you who resound with this restlessness, do not feel guilty or different. Anchoring in your own authentic self seems a far better solution than anchoring by the laws and beliefs of the changing terra firma.

18

Take Back Your Power

YES, middle-aged women do become more intolerant as they grow older…here is a list of things they would have uncomfortably tolerated in younger days, and are now having a late rebellion on…like a middle-aged rebel without a cause! Blame it on menopause or on a late realisation or just a general belated cumulative reaction…whatever the trigger is, here is the rant list.

- Will not share the bathroom.
- Will not be stared at or commented on by random hooligans on the road—either stare them down or shout out loud.
- Will not be coaxed out of that special holiday, dress, or luxurious jewellery we would like to gift ourself occasionally (alas, very few volunteered to buy one for us).
- Will not be a martyr Indian mom all the time, and definitely want to be nurtured right back.

- Will make automobile, housing, and sundry financial decisions independently, without being patronised or thought less sensible.
- Will not stay within an exclusive or elitist social group if we are not respected or treated as equals.
- Will no longer entertain family members or relatives who are misogynists or excruciatingly judgmental and demanding.
- Will not swallow the insult or refrain from expressing our true opinions in lieu of keeping the peace or the others' ego satisfied.
- Will call out in a rarefied work atmosphere when we disagree or have some particularly intelligent insights to offer.
- Will be open to offending esteemed clients who make ridiculous demands or interruptions.
- Will not go running to husbands/partners for the smallest of issues, let it be large or unmanageable enough to do it together, but we are no longer damsels in distress. On the other hand, we will gracefully accept all forms of help and chivalry if they are genuine offers from genuine men.
- Will cook as per mood and own wants too. Also we will demand that cooking to not be done alone or any housework for that matter. Can't believe even two decades later why this message doesn't go home. And no, it's not due to our failing health but because shared household chores brings the family closer.

After all, we are wiser and entitled to spread our wisdom even to those older to us.

After all, we are entitled to our pound of success along with promoting others' successes. If we may ask, others are welcome to promote our success and dreams too.

After all, we can encourage and support women as fellow travellers more so those who are off the grid or unconventional. To ensure that they are met with approval and not the societal norms of avoidance or passive acceptance.

19

Be and Stay a "Doer"

"Memory is not something you have; it is something you DO. Focus is not something you have; it is something you DO. Creativity is not something you have; it is something you DO. And so, you control it."

—Jim Kwik

So, here's my take on these words—the show must go on and you have to keep reinvesting in yourself. Yes, there is the fatigue of false starts, of failures and frustrations, and you are allowed to wallow for a while. It's okay to feel sorry, and sit like a sullen child waiting for the world to come to your rescue.

Here is the great news—your family will hear you for a while, love you and indulge you. The youngsters (maybe your grown-up children) may empathise, even understand and repose their faith in you, even if they are slightly bewildered by this slowdown from a strong pillar. Sometimes, it can be your friends who suddenly call you from nowhere, as if someone whispered in their heads: "Reach out, someone needs your help." Again, these are just gestures that the world has not given up on you, even while you take a temporary halt.

You bounce back, maybe with a little less spring in the step, and the bounce makes you touch your back gingerly, yet you do come back. If nothing else, life's experiences have told you that think, analyse, and plan—yes, all of that—but nothing is more exhilarating than action. Being the doer, the pace and the adrenalin of catching speed creates a momentum of its own. It makes the pulse beat faster, the blood rush, and each cell feels alive.

Once a doer, always a doer. If nothing else, at least we can learn this from the youth—they are always ready to try something new. They are ready to hear others, learn from others, grab the baton and run the race, and willing to take all the help they need. Outcomes are all that matter and so they happily accept whoever gives the push. Experiments, new learnings, open mind, and active listening—these are the attributes that we can definitely retain from our youth till we are lucid.

So, forgive and forget your mistakes, start over, keep the faith in yourself, and do not be a stick in the mud. Nothing, my friend, speaks more than action, and the world is observing and waiting for you to walk your talk.

Take the baton, do the work, and make it to the finish line of performance.

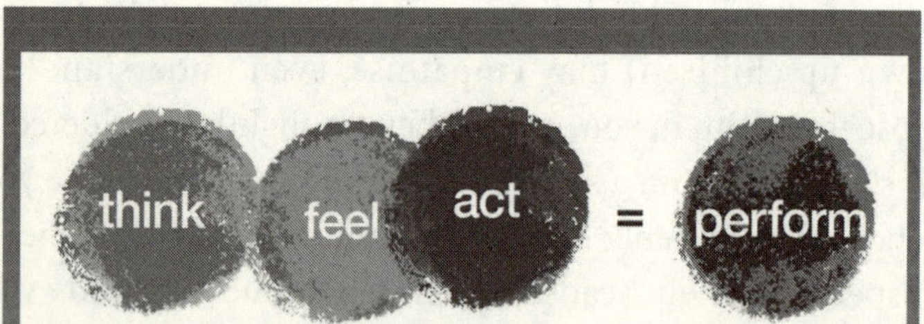

PART FOUR

THE GRAND FINALE: NUGGETS OF WISDOM

Dear 22-year-old Nandita,

Here are some pearls of wisdom to guide your way, so you don't repeat the mistakes of your older self. The world has two kinds of people—those that follow the trodden path and those who create their own. The latter will sound very glamourous, adventurous, and inspiring. Maybe it is all of these, and more. But (yes, life is full of buts), here is the catch—there are no free lunches.

You will hear and read a lot of hyperbole around "follow your passion", "fulfil your dreams", "believe in yourself—you will be unstoppable", etc. By all means, you should be inspired and happy reading these, but when you do make the decision to follow them, do remember to take the parachute. It is guaranteed that you will make mistakes, fall, almost give up, and have many other such stumbles and tumbles. Still, if you do have the tenacity to persist, become more flexible, find lateral ways or make mid-course corrections, and do not give up. Maybe, just maybe, you could stand tall and strong after all.

There are no magic, miracle, mantras, remedies, etc., that can help unless you are determined from within. If the fire in the belly dies, no inspiring quote or reading the biographies of great personalities will help. Fire means action towards success and not just dreaming of success. Therefore, there are only two pillars towards success—persistence and faith.

Persist with the goal, ensuring you learn as you fall; keep faith in yourself and the world that everybody does want you to succeed, and if that world can include your God, then by all means keep him in the loop too.

The second thing that I would have told my younger self without being cynical is—try not to look at the world with rose-coloured glasses. People do take a nice heart for a ride and, therefore, self-preservation is important. At the same time, there are some genuinely good people out there. Confusing, right? So, younger me, do not be overly cautious or overly foolish.

You know what, in the end I really just have one thing to say—follow your heart, but listen to your head. I know you will still make some mistakes and no one can stop you from doing so.

So, I wish you all the best and hope you have better safety nets that your older version had. Till then, don't worry, dear—I've got your back.

Dear Youngsters,

Re: Starts and beginning

As you stand on the brink of adulthood and working life, I see no better audience than you to distil the learnings I've squeezed till my midlife. As I cite these little nuggets of wisdom (I hope), I write to you not in any particular sequence or chronology of events. I write as the important milestones and dents of life appeared. About how they shaped and changed many of us in our middle-ages into what we have become—more settled, more thoughtful, and, hopefully, more evolved human beings who nevertheless remain naïve, dreamy, and out of touch with reality—a contrast that is guaranteed to make life interesting!

And therein lies the ***first nugget****—don't put off your dreams saying you have just started—start working on them now. For almost nothing will go according to plan and God knows you need time to tackle those curveballs, restarts, and detours.*

Dear Older Ones,

Re: Relationships

Looking back, we see a few episodes of having our hearts broken or even us breaking a few. In retrospect, maybe these incidents are small and insignificant, but they leave you feeling very guilty and incredibly sad about the long and lonely years, and a fear of having to venture again. Yet, we voyage this road again, with new hope and resurgence.

Growing up can be a bit lonely unless there are supporting and empathetic family and friends around who are concerned about your emotional wellbeing. Just a reassuring response of "everything will be alright, everything is fine" is often enough.

So dear sons and daughters,

Here is the ***second nugget.*** *As you stand on the brink of adulthood, do not take this age too seriously…it is a confusing time. Don't make it more confusing by withdrawing emotionally and trying to solve all your problems alone. God knows solitude is overrated and being open to help is not a sign of dependence but of trust. Take advice from people who practice what they preach and who value your happiness more than your agreement to their opinion.*

Dear Fledglings,

Re: True education

It is tragic how we run in the pursuit of power over all the other chases. We seek power through money, through law, through authority, through religion…the list is endless.

Talent does not equal success; people get attracted to success as a symbol of power, but do not appreciate the gift of talent. They celebrate and applaud those selected few who are showcased as successfully talented, which may owe less to the talent and more to the branding of it.

My ***third nugget*** *is, be true and passionate about your talent and interests, if you are lucky enough to have them or know them, then success will follow inevitably. Do not restrict yourself just because your path is unconventional and sees fewer successes. At the very least, you will earn enough to be happy, and the pursuit of your talent will anyway make you happy.*

Dear Growing Adults,

Re: Admiration of a few versus many

Think of the things that we undergo—the meltdowns of complete disappointments and the brave fronts that come to a grinding halt when all masks are pulled down. Despite all of this, I will still ask you to dream and imagine. However, the only caveat is that don't follow blindly, and only take on as much as you can cope with. If not the stars, sometimes just the nearest bright light does suffice. Not all of us are meant to shine in the sky; some can shine on the ground too. Doing something better, being different, being in the limelight.... these are paths to be tread on with caution. Do not dig yourself so deep into a hole that you are unable to come out of it. Moreover, it is true that even without public recognition, we are still uniquely precious. Ask families and friends, they will tell you how amazing you are and what they like about you. Receive their approval, bask in their love, and the rest of the world will not matter.

But if you feel that they are not enough, then rest assured, the world outside will also not be enough. Whether you are loved and admired by a few or many, it is the quality of the love that matters. The world outside will only see and admire your outcomes and success; it is the family who would have suffered with you and supported you in that journey. Hence, their admiration is more genuine than anyone else's, and I sincerely hope that will be enough for you.

By all means, have ambitions and expectations, but ensure you are also equally prepared for disappointments. You need to equip yourself with methods of coping and bouncing back.

Dear Hesitant Ones,

Re: Adaptability

The only adage that truly stands the test of time and struggles is "when life gives you lemons, make lemonade." Similar to that is "what you resist, persists." So, let go, be a little free flowing and make the best of current circumstances. That does not mean you compromise or subdue your natural zest and inclinations, but it does mean that evolve with changing situations and people.

Another ***nugget****—some of you may struggle to grow, to leave the nest, and may want to keep coming back like a homing pigeon. That is fine too. Give yourself time, there is no hurry. However, do know and accept that life is changing, you are changing, and people around you are changing. Enjoy the world outside even as you fly home. It is not a trade-off, but it certainly is making the most out of every moment. Belong to the moment where you are right now.*

Dear Almost Adults,

Re: Upon judging parents

As near grown-ups, you will start seeing your parents as the closest adults in your vicinity. I am sure, in fact, absolutely sure, that you will find us imperfect, inadequate, and faulty. You will no doubt question us, feel disappointed in us, and think we made some bad decisions.

We agree. In our defence, we can just say we did not know better and made decisions basis on what we knew and what made sense at that point in time. And yes, as you grow, we may start asking you for suggestions and weirdly you find yourself parenting us at times. It is not because we don't know parenting or are not sensible adults anymore, but maybe because the world around us has changed faster than we did. And, therefore, we expect you to be more in tune with the times.

None of us come equipped to handle unpredictable situations and our knowledge is limited to our past experiences. In hindsight, it is what you are using to evaluate us, the answers are very clear and obvious. But dears, do remember, both hindsight and foresight were not available to us at that time.

Here is wishing that you will learn from our mistakes and make fewer of your own....

Dear Young Adults,

Re: As you grow, we grow

Then comes the dreaded moment when your children become adolescents and you are forced to part with them, whether you are ready or not. You scream inside, "I am not ready!" but then are we ever ready as parents to let them fly? We worry, we are anxious, we hope the world is gentle with them, we cry when they cry, and through it all, we are only as happy as they are.

So this one is personal—from a mom to her grown-up children… and on behalf of all other moms who I am sure second these emotions.

Dear hearts of mine,

I don't even know how to begin this letter, so no nuggets in this one. I have no choice but to acknowledge that you both have grown-up, and I need to start letting go even more. I let go in pieces and now I let go some more as you start a life of your own with your own rules and values. All I can pray is that you will always be the man and woman of substance that I, hopefully, helped you become. That you will always be a human first and then a man and a woman, and that you will make your way in this world seamlessly.

I will always be around you, in your heart and just a call or visit away. At the slightest of bids, I will come running, disregarding money, effort, and time, not because you called me but because I need you too and always will. However, I will learn to cage that need, I will learn to restrain it so that it doesn't become a burden on you or on me.

In the end, it is only about the moments we live, the emotions we share, and the memories we create together. Neither time nor the world can snatch them away. I am content and grateful that I have been gifted with two angels, and I can share these gifts with the world now.

Lovingly yours,
Mom

.....More letters will follow as we watch you grow to your next phases and we will indeed try to catch up too, but here is a sneak preview....

Dear Newly Employed,

Re: The early working years

I always felt that my work life chose me, rather than the other way around. At the mercy of recruitment from my management school campus—close to what a young woman being dressed and adorned to be scrutinised by suitors for marriage would feel, we primed and presented ourselves to our would-be employers. We were anxious to impress and eager to outdo our classmates, the very friends we had spent the last two years with, in fun and harmony, now being jostled out on the competing line.

Companies came, we were discussed, interviewed, dissected, and analysed to "buy" the best… almost like we were cattle in a Farmer's fair! The lucky ones got selected first, the others waited for the second-best companies, and a few unlucky ones resigned to their fate of having a longer wait. Starting salaries were compared, egos were inflated and bruised, and each prepared for a new milestone in his/her life.

*I share my **next nugget** here. Our early working years are important. They help decide who you want to be and what you want to do for the rest of your life. It could be this or something completely different.*

Take the first thing that comes along, shower it with love and blessings, and see how it paves the way for success or a new direction. No opportunity is wrong, and no experience is without its merits. It's really that simple.

Yet do not fall default into a herd attitude. If supported financially or self-sufficient financially, make the early working years count and chose your path. Yes, it's frightening, but less so than the fear of being at the wrong place.

Holding your space, dears, as you figure it out.

Dear Working Adults,

Re: Planning your work journey…

At some point in time, you will think hard and wonder, should I be spending so much time and effort in building someone else's business or my own? It is inevitable and it will come. There will be a yearning to create something you can call your own or living life on your own terms.

Dear future entrepreneurs,

*A **nugget** to guide you on this journey—definitely this is a risky, roller coaster of a ride. Hold on tightly to the railings, and get into that ride. When you are on a high akin to the highest point of the giant wheel, the world will seem small, weary, with little men and women trudging along. Do not belittle them and be ready to rejoin their ranks, for like the giant wheel, you cannot stay on top forever. However, what will set you apart is the endurance with which you can stay low and rise to the top again. So do not give up whenever there is a low tide, wait it out, try new solutions, and stay the course.*

These are the parting lines of a song I do not remember—"catch a falling star, put it in your pocket, save it for a rainy day"—sing this line and use it as an umbrella for the rainy days.

Dear Working Adults,

Re: Eye to the sky and ear to the ground...

You may receive a lot of contradictory advice—some will tell you to tighten your belt now and save for the rainy days in the future. Others will tell you live for today, for life is short. Yet others might say enjoy life to the fullest.

So here is the ***nugget****, there is no one route—the only advice would be do what makes you feel good, along with hard work. Yet know that the future certainly is unpredictable, so regular savings during good times, prudential steps while taking loans, and creating budgets that include leisure are all good steps. Aim for the sky; be inspired and ambitious yet know that the world is not under your control. No need to tighten the belt, but do not create more holes in the belt either. In other words, fly but with straps firmly anchored to the ground.*

Dear Dating Adults,

Re: Partnering is work too…

When you do decide to marry or have a lifelong partner, remember that a large part of your happiness will depend on them. This includes how well you navigate it, which is one of the most important relationships. What makes this one harder than a blood relationship is that it cannot be taken for granted. It is a relationship made out of choice, so make your choices well, and once made, try your best to sustain it, nurture it, and make it bloom.

The next ***nugget****—do not forget why you chose a particular person to be your spouse or partner and do not play games or manipulate them. Being life-mates is a serious relationship and one deserving of efforts and respect, maybe even more than that accorded to work or external responsibilities. Though love is a lot about emotions, it is also a decision. Communication is the key and thresholds of tolerance have to be known and adhered to. Be flexible, give space, and keep ego very far away. Last but not the least, for heaven's sake, do not compare.*

Dear To-Be Parents,

Re: When you become parents…

Be ready for a tsunami of contradictions in you—exhilaration, fear, need to escape, sadness, and excitement, all at once, as you realise the enormity of being responsible for two tiny human beings, completely dependent on you in every way. To be honest, for some time, when you both were born, all I wanted was to be left alone to heal in peace. Even you, my dearests, did not appeal for the first few hours more than the need to recover….

But soon the floodgates of parental love and guilt opens, taking over like a storm. Ignoring your own pain and discomfort, you will walk every day two hours or more to help your child sleep.

You will beg your younger one, "At least you don't hurry to grow up and don't give in to the pressures of being less demonstrative."

All I know is that parenthood inspires in you the purest of feelings, from emotional love to soul love, as well as compassion and empathy as the child struggles to grow.

So here is a new ***nugget****, there is only one "heritage", "property", or "wealth", that you can give your kids and that is deep, undying love. You will always hope that the act of growing up will not create masks. Masks that make your children hide your attachments, that make them embarrassed to express their deepest feelings and make you artificially stoic. That is not strength. Strength comes from having the courage to be vulnerable—to expose the nakedness of your feelings in a world that is becoming more and more indifferent to emotions. Maybe it is better to be emotional fools than selfish takers.*

Cliches Revisited

NOW that I have more or less exhausted all dimensions of middle-age and rambled incoherently on them, I select some childhood adages and cliches and change them to reflect more on the middle-ages. All in good humour folks, as a grand finale to all my ramblings, revelations, and calls to action.

Existing cliche	Revised to...
A Jack of all trades is a master of none.	A Jack of all trades makes master of "some".
A bird in hand is worth two in the bush.	Two birds in hand is worthwhile, none in the bush!
Better safe than sorry.	Better brave than safe and sorry.
Nothing ventured, nothing gained.	Many ventures, some gains!
Actions speak louder than words.	Actions "last" longer than words.

Existing cliche	Revised to…
All work and no play makes Jack a dull boy.	All play and no work makes Jack a poor boy!
All's fair in love and war.	All's fair till one is winning and then it's war!
Don't bite off more than you can chew.	Do bite off more, but then chew quickly.
Don't burn all your bridges.	Burn all your bridges after you cross some.
When the going gets tough, the tough get going.	When the tough get going, the going gets rough!
Absence makes the heart grow fonder.	Absence makes the heart fond of another!
All that glitters is not gold.	All gold does not glitter either.
Any friend of yours is a friend of mine.	Any ***rich*** friend of yours is a friend of mine!
Ask not what your country can do for you, but what you can do for your country.	Ask not what your country can do for you, but what you can do for yourself!
Blood is thicker than water.	Water is what makes the blood!
Don't bite the hand that feeds you.	Don't feed the hand that bites you.
Don't rock the boat.	Rock the boat to move it
The more we learn, the less we know.	The more we experience, the more we learn.

Existing cliche	Revised to...
Ignorance is bliss.	Ignorance is a gap all rush to fill.
Penny saved is a penny earned.	Penny invested is a penny earned.
Pick the low hanging fruit.	Avoid the low hanging fruit that all can reach.
Nice guys finish last.	Nice guys finish last, but bad guys finish fast.
A rolling stone gathers no moss.	A stationary stone gathers only moss!
Only time will tell.	Time does tell, but do listen.
The writing's on the wall.	The "wall" creates the writings.
Take the tiger by its tail.	Observe the tiger's tail before you take it.
(There are) Plenty of fish in the sea.	Whales and piranhas too are fishes in the sea.
(Getting up) from the wrong side of the bed.	Getting out of bed has only wrong sides.

Truths I Learnt

Serve with service, not servility
Ask with humility, be grateful when you receive
Share your joy but do not appease
Believe your truths sans what others perceive
It is what it is, good or bad
Dream your wishes but plan for few
Your time will come, till then, take help
Bow to God, parents, and no one more
Sent to Earth as equals, our gifts vary
Some mark beginnings and some create endings
Life comes and goes in cycles, everything passes
Make roots with people but wander light as air
Reach your own truths, the purpose of being
Be weak, be vulnerable for what it reveals
Strength in acceptance, hands are extended
Cherish those who help, seeking none in return

Dear youth,

As we pass on the baton, here is one final nugget—some philosophy to guide you, based on own experiences, for knowledge comes not from information but from experiences...

'THERE'S NO HURRY ANYMORE WHEN ALL IS SAID AND DONE'

(ABBA)

Acknowledgment

MY biggest sources of inspiration have been the daily morning cup of coffee and the few plants that have managed to survive the hot Delhi sun. The combination just sets my brain into hyperdrive.

An equally important source has been my children—Mayank and Manasvi. My apologies, children; I know you wouldn't want your names stated in public, but your unflinching support has been too valuable to not be mentioned.

My editor brother who staunchly stood close by, as did my parents and family. I am grateful for all the fodder provided by the young and the old in the family! The extended intellectual South Indian family steadily accompanied me along the journey of writing, so thank you!

The third and very encouraging support has come from close-knit friends, middle-aged, of course, who have not only seen me grow from my college and working years but have also been cited in many tales of this book. I hope you recognise yourself there! A special thank you to the adventurous ones who have regaled me with their risk-taking stories.

Finally, a big shout of gratitude to the Nu Voice team—Kevin, Navya, Abhishek, Deepika, and the team for your patience, encouragement, and unstinting support in believing in my book and bringing it to life.

Thank you!

About the Author

Nandita has been working as a creative writer, blogger, and poet for over 10 years. She wrote her first short story and poem at the age of 9 and has had a steady relationship with the writing world since then. She describes herself on Medium.com as "A creative writer inspired by the highs and lows of life".

Her 25-odd years as a Consumer-Behaviour Specialist and Brand Planner have also given her insights into the corporate world. In contrast, her interests in healing, spiritual coaching, career coaching, and teaching management students have given her a broad base from which to approach diverse topics and mindsets. Her writing skills include content writing, articles, and blogs on non-fiction topics and her fiction pieces are currently underway in the drama and speculative genres.

Her writing services and skills may be seen in *Liquid Magazine* and *Medium.com*. She has also been published in *Kaleidoscope*, an anthology of short stories by *StoryMirror.com*.